Beginning Latin II

Answer Key

Written by Margaret Hayden
Cover art by Claire Yanoschik
Chapter art by Lisa Berquist

© 2016 Mother of Divine Grace School - Revised June 2018

Manufactured by Thomson-Shore, Dexter, MI (USA); RMA24LS084, June, 2018

❦ Beginning Latin II ❦

INTRODUCTION

In the first lesson, students are introduced to the two essential parts of a sentence: the noun and the verb. This lesson is formal, as students are given definitions which they will memorize and practice. As the noun is easier to understand in use than the verb, the lessons continue by providing more formal terms for verbs. The goal of this is to help the young student understand that verbs are "complicated" and have many aspects that must be explored. Following this first lesson, then, students delve into verbs.

Most courses will give the students verbs in paradigms – amo, amas, amat…. – or will have the students learn endings first – o, s, t…. – In Beginning Latin, before jumping into these endings or paradigms, students spend a great deal of time on the parts of verbs (endings and stems). Most Latin programs do not focus on the parts of a verb adequately, which in my experience leaves students guessing as to how to combine the ending and stem. Before understanding that verbs can be conjugated, they must understand that the verbs have parts so that conjugation can be done correctly.

Decoding

I introduce endings and stems next because of my experience teaching Latin to students. Knowing how to build a Latin verb on a stem has been a constant problem and one I particularly aimed to correct in writing this program. You can't know the whole in a distinct manner if you don't know the parts. Additionally, students need universal rules regarding common features in order to determine what conjugation a verb belongs in. Learning verbs separately (which is what students often do) creates unnecessary work for the young student and doesn't help later when the students reach a higher level where quick recognition of parts is needed. In this program, after recognizing the parts, students are asked to find the commonalities. This is why we progress next to grouping into "conjugations". Once students have conjugations, they can learn rules for conjugating in different tenses. This is the time to introduce past, present and future. For the sake of the young student's understanding, what is commonly called the 'imperfect' is called the 'past' here. This will not cause trouble later because we don't use the term 'perfect' until we introduce complete actions. Students are in fact learning a past tense when they learn the imperfect, it is just the past of ongoing actions. Students are taught this so they can later make the logical distinction between complete and ongoing actions and recognize they each have a past, present and future. It will only be by understanding what we call the "Present System" in the light of ongoing actions that the tense use becomes clear. Similarly, the "Perfect System" is for complete actions. Students who understand the purpose and true difference between these systems now will be more precise translators later.

These are strange verbs

It is also worth noting that this is the only program I know of where the irregular verbs are taught right away as are the third and fourth conjugation. This is because many of the irregular verbs are fundamental to knowing Latin well. Memorizing them while young is best, for children have the greatest faculty for memorization. (We start by memorizing the Latin only, and then add the English meanings – thus, the emphasis is on memorization, not understanding, yet.) We focus on the third conjugation for a simple reason. Most Latin verbs are in this conjugation. So if you want to read Latin later you need to know the third conjugation really well. Students who learn the first and second conjugation first have trouble identifying the "e" + ending as a future. They think of future as the "bo, bis, bit" words. This causes a great deal of trouble in later Latin. The fourth is learned after the third because it is so similar to the third that it is easy to remember.

Synopsis

I often ask the students to do a synopsis. This means to give a word in the same person (1st, 2nd, or 3rd) and number (singular or plural) for all tenses, moods and voices. This should precede conjugation because it is building the file folder in the brain into which the information is sorted. An orderly mind, capable of memorizing and recalling Latin will have the file folders where one must look clearly labeled.

Future Possible

I am sure very few of you have ever heard this term. It is my name for the subjunctive present. The present subjunctive has a sense of possibility and in that way (that is why) it is like the future indicative (indicative is the mood used for facts.) The whole goal is help students see that the subjunctive present is like the regular indicative futures and that the subjunctive has a sense of potentiality.

Nouns

Nouns are taught through observing their uses in sentences. Students begin by learning the third declension, rather than the first or second. Again, this is because there are far more words in the third declension than in the other declensions. Familiarity with the words from the largest category of words makes reading the language much easier. Noun use is practiced through sentence translations. Students also learn how to build nouns on their stems, how to identify the stems, and the English name equivalents of the Latin cases.

Learning Latin

Students are encouraged to use flashcards and do oral drill with mom. The program, though, is set up for a student to just work through the worksheets on his own. Students who do this will learn the vocabulary despite lack of formal study because no new words are introduced after about Week 16 or so. This gives the student time to practice.

❧ Table of Contents ❧

Lesson I ~ Nouns, Verbs, Sentences and Verb Stems	pg. 1
Lesson II ~ Singular and Plural, Personal Endings for Verbs, Four Conjugations	pg. 6
Lesson III ~ How to form Tenses for Verbs, Synopsis in Present, Imperfect, and Future	pg. 10
Lesson IV ~ Nouns in Latin, Gender and Case Endings; Sentences in Three Tenses	pg. 15
Lesson V ~ How to tell Nouns from Verbs in Latin; Simple Latin Sentence (subject and verb)	pg. 21
Lesson VI ~ Nominative (subject) case, and Genitive (possessive) case	pg. 28
Lesson VII ~ Latin Sentences with Nominative and Genitive; Accusative (direct object) case	pg. 35
Lesson VIII ~ Nominative, Genitive, and Accusative Case Endings, 4th Conjugation Verbs; Introduction of the Future Possible	pg. 44
Review Lesson A ~ Synopsis, Irregular Verbs, Finding Stems, translating verb tenses including the Future Possible	pg. 54
Lesson IX ~ Prepositions; Building Complex Latin Sentences	pg. 62
Lesson X ~ More with Genitives (Possessives) and the Future Possible	pg. 72
Lesson XI ~ Introduction of the Dative (indirect object) Case	pg. 82
Lesson XII ~ Purpose and the Dative Case; Review of Four Cases; Sentences with the Dative	pg. 93
Lesson XIII ~ Prepositions with Ablative and Accusative; Sentences with Prepositions	pg. 104
Lesson XIV ~ Review of Five Cases	pg. 115
Lesson XV ~ Analyzing Sentences for all Five Cases; i-stem Nouns	pg. 126
Lesson XVI ~ Review of Case and Gender; more on i-stem Nouns	pg. 135
Review Lesson B ~ Synopsis, Finding Stems, Tense endings	pg. 145
Lesson XVII ~ Practice identifying Genders and Case Endings; Sentence Analysis	pg. 158
Lesson XVIII ~ Plural endings for Nouns in all Five Cases	pg. 166
Lesson XIX ~ Sentence Analysis, Practice with Plurals	pg. 174
Lesson XX ~ Review of Gender, Singular and Plural Case Endings, and Verb Synopsis	pg. 181
Lesson XXI ~ Further Review	pg. 188
Lesson XXII ~ Singular and Plural Case Endings for i-stem Nouns	pg. 196
Lesson XXIII ~ 4th Conjugation Verb Synopsis with Future Possible	pg. 204
Lesson XXIV ~ Review	pg. 211
Review Lesson C ~ Tenses and Verb synopsis; Case, Gender and Number for Nouns	pg. 219

Lesson I
ఎంఓ

VOCABULARY:

laudare	to praise	**monēre**	to warn
audire	to hear	**agere**	to act, to do
bibere	to drink	**edere**	to eat
ponere	to put, to place	**regere**	to rule
vivere	to live	**vincere**	to conquer

In English, when you want to convey something you need a <u>noun</u> and a <u>verb</u>.

What is a sentence? Well, it comes from the Latin word *sententia* which means "opinion". *Sententia* is related to the verb *sentire* which means "to feel". So a sentence is a unit; it's a sequence of words that together tells us something (assertion), asks us something (question), or tells us to DO something (command).

Why are sentences important? Try not using a sentence but ask your mom for a cookie! Does it work? If so, how did you convey the idea?

The building blocks of a sentence are the <u>noun</u> and the <u>verb</u>.

A noun names a person, place, or thing.

A verb is a word that is capable of asserting something.

Day 1, Exercise 1: Use your chart to answer the questions:

What is a noun? ***A noun names a person, place, or thing.***

What is a verb? ***A verb is a word that is capable of asserting something.***

Day 1, Exercise 2: Divide the words into nouns and verbs. Write these words in the correct column:

do, run, lead, drink, rule, put, United States, fall, believe, bread, tree, sun, foot, warn, farmer, wolf, kitchen, Lucia, house, story, star, village, Italy

Nouns	Verbs
United States	do
bread	run
tree	lead
sun	drink
foot	rule
farmer	put
wolf	fall
kitchen	believe
Lucia	warn
house	
story	
star	
village	
Italy	

Day 2, Exercise 1: Take the list of words that are in your "NOUN" box and divide them up into nouns that name persons, places or things.

Person	Place	Thing
farmer	*United States*	*bread*
Lucia	*kitchen*	*tree*
	Italy	*sun*
		foot
		wolf
		house
		story
		star
		village

In English we make a complete sentence by putting a noun used as the subject of the sentence and a verb together. But in Latin, it's already done! Each verb has what we call the stem, followed by the "sign" of the "tense" and then by the "ending". So, let's review these terms:

STEM

This is the part of the sentence on which one builds the rest. It's like the stem of a plant.

TENSE

This is the part of the sentence that indicates if the verb is expressing the present *time*, past *time* or future *time/possibility*. We will talk more about this later.

ENDING

This indicates if the verb is first person, second person, or third person.

STEM: To find the stem, you need to drop the -re on what we will call the indeterminate or infinitive form (After all, we have almost "infinite" possibilities for sentences once we have the infinitive form):

Example - Laudare - re = lauda (lauda is the stem)

Day 2, Exercise 2: You find the stem of the vocabulary words:

1) laudare
   - re
   ──────
   lauda

2) *monēre*
   - re
   ──────
   monē

3) *audire*
   - re
   ──────
   audi

4) *agere*
   - re
   ──────
   age

5) *bibere*
   - re
   ──────
   bibe

6) *edere*
   - re
   ──────
   ede

7) *vivere*
   - re
   ──────
   vive

8) *ponere*
   - re
   ──────
   pone

9) *regere*
   - re
   ──────
   rege

10) *vincere*
    - re
    ──────
    vince

Some verbs show us an action. Other verbs link two things. So, the verb "run", for example, shows us an action. "Mary runs." is a sentence. The verb "is", on the other hand, links two words "Mary is happy". It linked "Mary" and "happy".

Day 3, Exercise 1: Build sentences using the list of words in Exercise 2. Plus you are allowed to use "a", "an", and "the". What do you notice about your sentences?
(Answers will vary)

1.

2.

3.

4.

Do you think you used linking verbs or action verbs? ***Action verbs***

Sentences can tell us something in different ways. Most sentences just state a fact or just tell us something (assertion). However, some sentences tell us to DO something (command). We call these command sentences. The Latin name for command sentences is imperative. It comes from the Latin word "to command". It's easy to remember because it sounds like "emperor", doesn't it? And emperors command! In Latin we call assertion sentences, indicatives. The root word "dico" means "to speak".

Day 3, Exercise 2: Well, what is each sentence telling us? Match each sentence with the correct answer:

Eat cake, Mary! ***(Command/Imperative)***   Assertion/Indicative

Mary eats cake.   ***(Assertion/Indicative)***   Command/Imperative

Lesson II
ಬಿಃಆ

laudare	to praise	monēre	to warn
audire	to hear	agere	to act, to do
bibere	to drink	edere	to eat
ponere	to put, to place	regere	to rule
vivere	to live	vincere	to conquer

In Latin, the words "a", "an", and "the" are not translated. So, when you are translating from English to Latin ignore them and when you are translating for Latin to English add them as needed.

Day 1, Exercise 1: Cross out the words "a", "an", and "the".

It is proper to say ~~a~~ prayer of adoration. ~~A~~ popular prayer to say is ~~a~~ "Glory Be". Glory be to ~~the~~ Father and to ~~the~~ Son and to ~~the~~ Holy Spirit. As it was in ~~the~~ beginning, is now, and ever will be. Amen.

In English and Latin, we refer to one of something as SINGULAR and more than one of something as PLURAL.

Day 1, Exercise 2: Indicate whether the following words are singular by writing an "s" after them, or plural by writing a "p" after them. (Hint: One of these can be singular AND plural.)

1) dog _S_
2) mice _P_
3) brushes _P_
4) women _P_
5) grass _S or P_
6) dinners _P_
7) goat _S_
8) bird _S_

> **In Latin, there are some very basic endings:**
>
> | | | | | |
> |---|---|---|---|---|
> | -o, or -m | I | | -mus | we |
> | -s | you (sing) | | -tis | you (pl) |
> | -t | he, she, or it* | | -nt | they |
>
> *Decide from context about whether to use "he", or "she", or "it" for the Latin "t". If there are no clues in the sentence, use "he".

Do you know that I, you, he, she, it, we, you, and they express the person?

"I" and "we" are first person because they express the speaker's personal perspective. "You" is second person because it expresses the person to whom the speaker is talking.

"He, she, it," and "they" are third person because the speaker is talking about a third person. The speaker is not talking about himself or directly to someone.

Day 2, Exercise 1: Fill in the blanks with the correct answer.

1) The Latin ending that means "we" in English is __*mus*__ in Latin.

2) What Latin ending means "he", "she", or "it" in English? __*t*__

3) If you were telling your whole family something like "You all need to start school.", would you use "-tis" or "s" for "You?__*tis*__ (HINT: You are talking to many people not to a single person. Which "you" should be used for many people?)

Day, 2, Exercise 2: Give the person (1, 2, or 3) of each of these pronouns. Also, say if they are Singular or Plural (You can use "S" for singular and "P" for plural.) I did the first one for you:

I	*1, S*		We	*1, P*
You	*2, S*		You	*2, P*
He, She, It	*3, S*		They	*3, P*

Day 3, Exercise 1: Look at the following words. They mean, "am, is, are". Circle the ending part of each word and then translate. Choose whatever meaning "am, is, are" sounds best to put with the ending:

sum	*I am*	sumus	*We are*
es	*You are*	estis	*You are*
est	*He is**	sunt	*They are*

**If there is no hint in the sentence as to whether to use he, she, or it, use he.*

In English, we usually put the subject before the verb. For example, we say:

You live. *YOU* is the subject.

Latin word order is different. For example, the endings are at the end of the words, which means that the you comes after the verb word itself.

"Laudas" in Latin is lauda (praise) + s (you). So, the you is after the praise. But when we put it into good English, we put the you first so we sound normal. Think about how strange it would be if we didn't change the word order. It would sound like this:

Eat you the cake. Tastes the cake yummy.

Conjugations are particular groupings of like verbs in Latin.

Look at all the words in your vocabulary list again. In it, the words can be broken down into four conjugations. Look at the conjugations of the words:

Vocabulary:

laudare	to praise	FIRST CONJUGATION
monēre	to warn	SECOND CONJUGATION
audire	to hear	FOURTH CONJUGATION
agere	to act, to do	THIRD CONJUGATION

(Continued on the next page.)

bibere	**to drink**	THIRD CONJUGATION
edere	**to eat**	THIRD CONJUGATION
vivere	**to live**	THIRD CONJUGATION
ponere	**to put, to place**	THIRD CONJUGATION
regere	**to rule**	THIRD CONJUGATION
vincere	**to conquer**	THIRD CONJUGATION

Day 3, Exercise 2: What determines the conjugation of the verb? (Hint: Look at the letter before the final "re"). Now fill in the blanks:

1) First Conjugation words have an *a* before the "-re".

2) *Second* Conjugation words haven an "é" before the "-re".

3) *Third* Conjugation words haven an "e" before the "-re".

4) Fourth Conjugation words have an *i* before the "-re".

Lesson III
ଽଠଓଃ

laudare (1st Conjugation)   to praise

monēre (2nd Conjugation)   to warn

audire (4th Conjugation)   to hear

agere   (3rd Conjugation)   to act, to do

bibere (3rd Conjugation)   to drink

edere   (3rd Conjugation)   to eat

vivere (3rd Conjugation)   to live

ponere (3rd Conjugation)   to put, to place

regere (3rd Conjugation)   to rule

vincere (3rd Conjugation)   to conquer

Last class you learned these endings and what they mean. Review them.

In Latin, there are some very basic endings:			
-o, or -m	I	-mus	we
-s	you (sing)	-tis	you
-t	he, she, or it	-nt	they

Memorize this: sum, es, est, sumus, estis, sunt

Day 1, Exercise 1: Write out what these words mean.

sum   *I am*   sumus   *we are*

es   *you are*   estis   *you are*

est   *he is*   sunt   *they are*

Day 1, Exercise 2: Cross out the three words below from the vocabulary that are different than the others. (Hint: Look at the letter before the final "re").

Vocabulary:

~~laudare~~	vivere	vincere	ponere
~~audire~~	agere	~~monēre~~	regere
bibere	edere		

We are going to learn about the tenses of the present system. Remember what was said about tense before?

TENSE

This is the part of the sentence that indicates if the verb is expressing the present *time*, past *time* or future *time/possibility*.

There are three ways to express these tenses:

First, express what is happening right now.	*You eat cake.*
	You are eating cake.
Second, express what began in the past.	*You were eating cake.*
Third, express what will happen in the future	*You will eat cake.*

How do you say this in Latin? (I am going to leave the word "cake" in English for now.)

First, express what is happening right now.	*Edis cake. You eat cake.*
	Edis cake. You are eating cake.
Second, express what began in the past.	*Edébas cake. You were eating cake*
Third, express what will happen in the future	*Edes cake. You will eat cake.*

So now we can see something interesting:

> To state something in the present, which is what is happening right now, take the stem of the word, change the final "e" of the stem to "i" and add the ending. To state something that began in the past, take the stem of the word, change the "e" to a long "é" and then add "ba" plus the ending. To form the future, something that will happen in the future or is possible, just add the personal endings to the stem.

Day 2, Exercise 1: Are the following statements true or false?

1) __True__   A past tense expresses what began in the past.

2) __False__   A future tense expresses what is happening right now.

3) __True__   A future tense expresses possibility.

4) __True__   When you state "Mary eats cake," you are speaking in the present tense.

Day 2, Exercise 2: Cross out the stem and underline the ending:

~~ede~~<u>s</u>   ~~vive~~<u>bas</u>   ~~bibe~~<u>bas</u>

~~agi~~<u>s</u>   ~~age~~<u>s</u>   ~~poni~~<u>s</u>

Day 3, Exercise 1: You observed that to state something in the present, which is what is happening right now, take the stem of the word, change the final "e" of the stem to "i" and add the ending. Please translate the following words as present. Remember "s" means "you" (sing).

edi + s = __You eat or You are eating__

vivi + s = __You live or You are living__

agi + s = __You do (act) or You are doing (acting)__

bibi + s = __You drink or You are drinking__

poni + s = __You put (place) or You are putting (placing)__

Day 3, Exercise 2: Synopsis and give the meaning of all words in the "e" conjugation. Here they are:

agere	to act, to do	ponere	to put, to place
bibere	to drink	regere	to rule
edere	to eat	vincere	to conquer
vivere	to live		

Here's an example of a synopsis:

agis	you act
agebas	you were acting
ages	you will act

Word	Meaning
bibis	you drink
bibebas	you were drinking
bibes	you will drink

Word	Meaning
edis	you eat
edebas	you were eating
edes	you will eat

Word	Meaning
vivis	you live
vivebas	you were living
vives	you will live

(This exercise is continued on the next page.)

Word	Meaning
ponis	*you put (place)*
ponebas	*you were putting (placing)*
pones	*you will put (place)*

Word	Meaning
regis	*you rule*
regebas	*you were ruling*
reges	*you will rule*

Word	Meaning
vincis	*you conquer*
vincebas	*you were conquering*
vinces	*you will conquer*

Lesson IV
ಬ‌ಡ

Go over these every day for 5 minutes. New words are in bold.

laudare	to praise	**credere**	**to believe**
monēre	to warn	**ducere**	**to lead**
audire	to hear	**currere**	**to run**
agere	to act, to do	**mittere**	**to send**
bibere	to drink	**defendere**	**to defend**
edere	to eat	**scribere**	**to write**
vivere	to live	**sentire**	**to feel**
ponere	to put, to place	**munire**	**to build**
regere	to rule	**dicere**	**to say**
vincere	to conquer		

Make sure you memorize the following.

-o, or -m	I	-mus	we
-s	you (sing)	-tis	you
-t	he, she or it	-nt	they

sum, es, est, sumus, estis, sunt *(I am, you are, he is, we are, you are, they are)*

eram, eras, erat, eramus, eratis, erant *(I was, you were, he was, we were, you were, they were)**

ero, eris, erit, erimus, eritis, erunt *(I will be, you will be, he will be, we will be, you will be, they will be)**

possum, potes, potest, possumus, potestis, possunt *(I am able, you are able, he is able, we are able, you are able, they are able)*

*Just memorize these words and their meanings for now.

Beginning Latin II - Lesson IV

Day 1, Exercise 1: Can you fill in the blanks with the missing words?

sum   *es*   est   *sumus*   estis   sunt

Day 1, Exercise 2: Apply what you know about endings to this new word. This new words means "am able, is able, are able." So, underline the ending and give the meaning of the ending. After you underline the ending and write down its meaning, use whatever sounds best from among: "am able, is able, are able."

possu<u>m</u>	*I am able*	po<u>ssumus</u>	*we are able*
pote<u>s</u>	*you are able*	po<u>testis</u>	*you are able*
pot<u>est</u>	*he is able*	po<u>ssunt</u>	*they are able*

Day 2, Exercise 1: Synopsis and give the meaning of these words from the "e" conjugation.

agere	to act, to do
bibere	to drink
edere	to eat
vivere	to live

You did this synopsis of the verbs last week in second person singular (that means the "s" ending.) Now I want you do the exact same thing in 3rd person singular. So, that means instead of adding an "s" you will add a "t".

Here's the synopsis of "agere":

agit	**he acts**
agebat	**he was acting**
aget	**he will act**

(This exercise is continued on the next page.)

Word	Meaning
bibit	he drinks
bibebat	he was drinking
bibet	he will drink

Word	Meaning
edit	he eats
edebat	he was eating
edet	he will eat

Word	Meaning
vivit	he lives
vivebat	he was living
vivet	he will live

Now take these verbs:

agere   to act, to do

ponere   to put, to place

regere   to rule

vincere   to conquer

(This exercise is continued on the next page.)

Give a synopsis of these verbs in 1st person plural. So, that means you will add a "mus".

Here's the synopsis of "agere":

        agimus   we act

        agebamus   we were acting

        agemus   we will act

Word	Meaning
ponimus	*we put (place)*
ponebamus	*we were putting (placing)*
ponemus	*we will put (place)*

Word	Meaning
regimus	*we rule*
regebamus	*we were ruling*
regemus	*we will rule*

Word	Meaning
vincimus	*we conquer*
vincebamus	*we were conquering*
vincemus	*we will conquer*

Day 2, Exercise 2: What ending would you add to each of these words?

You rule   regi + **s**   He acts   agi + **t**

He puts   poni + **t**   We live   vivi + **mus**

Day 3, Exercise 1: Can you identify the tense of these verbs? Some are in Latin and some are in English.

A. I was calling. *(Past)*

B. I will bring. *(Future)*

C. I am eating. *(Present)*

D. I rule. *(Present)*

E. Regis. *(Present)*

F. Reget. *(Future)*

G. Regebat. *(Past)*

H. Vincet. *(Future)*

I. Vincebamus. *(Past)*

J. Agitis. *(Present)*

1. Present
2. Past
3. Future
4. Present
5. Present
6. Future
7. Past
8. Past
9. Present
10. Future

Day 3, Exercise 2: Remember that you have been doing a synopsis of your verbs. I have a complete synopsis here for the verb "regere."

	Present	Past	Future
1st Singular	rego*	regebam	regam*
2nd Singular	regis	regebas	reges
3rd Singular	regit	regebat	reget
1st Plural	regimus	regebamus	regemus
2nd Plural	regitis	regebatis	regetis
3rd Plural	regunt*	regebant	regent

*These forms don't follow the regular rules. Memorize them.

(This exercise is continued on the next page.)

Now you do a synopsis of "vivere". The gray shading is to remind you that these forms are the ones that are different and need to be memorized.

	Present	Past	Future
1st Singular	vivo	vivebam	vivam
2nd Singular	vivis	vivebas	vives
3rd Singular	vivit	vivebat	vivet
1st Plural	vivimus	vivebamus	vivemus
2nd Plural	vivitis	vivebatis	vivetis
3rd Plural	vivunt	vivebant	vivent

Lesson V

൸൚

Go over these every day for 5 minutes. New words are in bold.

laudare	to praise	sentire	to feel
monēre	to warn	munire	to build
audire	to hear	dicere	to say
agere	to act, to do	**dolor, doloris**	**pain, sorrow**
bibere	to drink	**panis, panis**	**bread**
edere	to eat	**mons, montis**	**mountain**
vivere	to live	**crux, crucis**	**cross**
ponere	to put, to place	**homo, hominis**	**man**
regere	to rule	**urbs, urbis**	**city**
vincere	to conquer	**flumen, fluminis**	**river**
credere	to believe	**civitas, civitatis**	**state**
ducere	to lead	**pax, pacis**	**peace**
currere	to run	**caput, capitis**	**head**
mittere	to send	**Caesar, Caesaris**	**Caesar**
defendere	to defend	**Cicero, Ciceronis**	**Cicero**
scribere	to write		

Make sure you memorize the following.

-o, or -m	I	-mus	we
-s	you (sing)	-tis	you
-t	he, she, or it	-nt	they

sum, es, est, sumus, estis, sunt *(I am, you are, he is, we are, you are, they are)*

eram, eras, erat, eramus, eratis, erant *(I was, you were, he was, we were, you were, they were)*

ero, eris, erit, erimus, eritis, erunt *(I will be, you will be, he will be, we will be, you will be, they will be)*

possum, potes, potest, possumus, potestis, possunt *(I am able, you are able, he is able, we are able, you are able, they are able)*

poteram, poteras, poterat, poteramus, poteratis, poterant *(I was able, you were able, he was able, we were able, you were able, they were able)*

potero, poteris, poterit, poterimus, poteritis, poterunt *(I will be able, you will be able, he will be able, we will be able, you will be able, they will be able)*

Day 1, Exercise 1: Fill in these charts.

	First	Second	Third
Singular	sum	es	*est*
Plural	*sumus*	estis	*sunt*

	First	Second	Third
Singular	eram	eras	*erat*
Plural	*eramus*	*eratis*	erant

	First	Second	Third
Singular	poteram	poteras	*poterat*
Plural	*poteramus*	*poteratis*	poterant

Until this week, every word in your vocabulary has been a verb. This week you were introduced to noun forms. Nouns have stems too. I have put the stems in bold. **Remember:**

A noun names a person, place or thing.			

dolor, **dolor**is	pain, sorrow	flumen, **flumin**is	river
panis, **pan**is	bread	civitas, **civitat**is	state
mons, **mont**is	mountain	pax, **pac**is	peace
crux, **cruc**is	cross	caput, **capit**is	head
homo, **homin**is	man	Caesar, **Caesar**is	Caesar
urbs, **urb**is	city	Cicero, **Ciceron**is	Cicero

Memorize these nouns. Also, notice that they all have very different first forms but the second forms all end in "-is". The stem is everything before the "-is". This is similar to verbs where the stem was everything before the "-re".

A verb is a word that is capable of asserting something.
A noun names a person, place or thing.

How can you tell a noun from a verb in Latin? Well, there are two keys.

First, when you hear a word in Latin, you probably remember what it means in English. Think of that English meaning and remember what a noun and verb are. Does the English word tell us about a person, place or thing? If so, it's a noun. And, if it's a noun in English, it's one in Latin too. Does the word assert something in English? If so, it's a verb in English and one in Latin too.

Second, most verbs have the ending with -are, -ēre, -ere, or -ire. So that would be another sign that a word is a verb. But let's take an example, "ponis" is a verb, but some nouns can have an "is" ending, like "panis". So, in a case like this you have to go back to the word in its form that you memorized it in. So, you know "ponis" is from "ponere" and since "ponere" ends in "-ere", you know it's a verb. Also, if you think about the meaning of the word in English "to put" you realize that's a verb — a word that asserts something — not a noun — a person, place or thing.

Day 1, Exercise 2: Remember that you can find stems for both nouns and verbs. Identify the words as nouns or verbs. (I did the first few.) And then write the stem.

1. regere	*__Verb__*	*__rege__*
2. homo, hominis	*__Noun__*	*__homin__*
3. credere	*__Verb__*	*__crede__*
4. flumen, fluminis	*__Noun__*	*__flumin__*
5. caput, capitis	*__Noun__*	*__capit__*
6. audire	*__Verb__*	*__audi__*
7. bibere	*__Verb__*	*__bibe__*
8. dolor, doloris	*__Noun__*	*__dolor__*

Nouns have gender. Gender means that the words are designated as masculine (male), feminine (female) or neuter (neutral) based on some characteristic of the object. Here are the ways you can tell if the nouns we have learned so far are masculine, feminine, or neuter. Look at the first form of the word:

Feminine nouns usually end in s-o-x

Neuter nouns usually end in l-a-n-c-e-t

Masculine nouns end in er-r-or

So, a word like "dolor" is masculine because it ends in "or" which is included in er-r-or. A word like "flumen" is neuter because it ends in "n" which is included in l-a-n-c-e-t.

However, there are always some exceptions. For example, the word "Cicero" would be feminine according to the s-o-x rule, but it's masculine because it names a male person. That's the biggest exception: words that clearly denote a person of a particular gender are in that gender. Also, the word "mons" would be feminine according to the rule, but it's masculine. I guess the Romans thought that mountains were masculine because they were tall and powerful.

(Continued on the next page.)

Finally, the word "panis" is masculine, even though, again, it should be feminine according to the s-o-x rule. In this case, the word "panis" comes from a Latin verb "pasco". Words that come from verbs are often masculine. For now, it will be best to memorize exceptions. In future weeks you will see this noted in the vocabulary after exceptions, like this:

panis, panis (m) bread

The "m" is for masculine. For a word like "dolor", since it is masculine based on the er-r-or rule, there will be no gender noted:

dolor, doloris suffering

Day 2, Exercise 1: Apply the rules to come up with the gender of the following nouns:

1. dolor — *masculine (er-r-or)*
2. crux — *feminine (s-o-x)*
3. urbs — *feminine (s-o-x)*
4. flumen — *neuter (l-a-n-c-e-t)*
5. civitas — *feminine (s-o-x)*
6. pax — *feminine (s-o-x)*
7. caput — *neuter (l-a-n-c-e-t)*

Day 2, Exercise 2: Remember that you have been doing a synopsis of your verbs. I have a complete synopsis here for the verb "regere."

	Present	Past	Future
1st Singular	rego*	regebam	regam*
2nd Singular	regis	regebas	reges
3rd Singular	regit	regebat	reget
1st Plural	regimus	regebamus	regemus
2nd Plural	regitis	regebatis	regetis
3rd Plural	regunt*	regebant	regent

*These forms don't follow the regular rules. Memorize them.

Now you do a synopsis of "credere". The gray shading is to remind you that these forms are the ones that are different and need to be memorized.

	Present	Past	Future
1st Singular	credo	credebam	credam
2nd Singular	credis	credebas	credes
3rd Singular	credit	credebat	credet
1st Plural	credimus	credebamus	credemus
2nd Plural	creditis	credebatis	credetis
3rd Plural	credunt	credebant	credent

Remember:

A sentence is a unit; it's a sequence of words that together tells us something (assertion), asks something (question) or tells us to DO something (command).

Day 3, Exercise 1: Follow directions below.

Write a sentence in the future tense:

(Answers may vary)

Write a sentence in the past tense:

(Answers may vary)

Write a sentence in the present tense:

(Answers may vary)

Let's learn about subjects. **A subject is a particular way to use a noun**. A noun names a person, place or thing. To use a noun as a subject is to make it the main thing talked about in the sentence. So, in the following sentences I have underlined the subjects.

I want to go with you.

John and Mary went to the movie.

Five dollars was a lot of money in 1806.

The best way to test to see if you found it is to ask yourself "who" or "what" in regards to the verb. You remember, verbs, right? They are the words that assert something.

Here is how to test for them. The verbs are double underlined.

I want to go with you.	*Who* wants to go?	The answer is the subject, I.
John and Mary went to the movie.	*Who* went to the movie?	The answer is the subject, John and Mary
Five dollars was a lot of money in 1806.	*What* was a lot of money in 1806?	The answer is the subject, five dollars.

Day 3, Exercise 2: Now you find the subjects in these sentences:

1. I hear a noise. Subject: ***I***

Test this: Who hears a noise? ***I*** (Your answer is the subject.)

2. Caesar ate the bread Subject: ***Caesar***

Test this: Who ate the bread? ***Caesar*** (Your answer is the subject.)

3. Cicero believed Caesar. Subject: ***Cicero***

Test this: Who believed Caesar? ***Cicero*** (Your answer is the subject.)

4. Did you eat cake too? Subject: ***You***

Test this: Who does eat the cake too? ***You*** (Your answer is the subject.)

Lesson VI

Go over these every day for 5 minutes. New words are in bold.

laudare	to praise	dolor, doloris	pain, sorrow
monēre	to warn	panis, panis (m)	bread
audire	to hear	mons, montis (m)	mountain
agere	to act, to do	crux, crucis	cross
bibere	to drink	homo, hominis (m)	man
edere	to eat	urbs, urbis	city
vivere	to live	flumen, fluminis	river
ponere	to put, to place	civitas, civitatis	state
regere	to rule	pax, pacis	peace
vincere	to conquer	caput, capitis	head
credere	to believe	Caesar, Caesaris	Caesar
ducere	to lead	Cicero, Ciceronis (m)	Cicero
currere	to run	**canis, canis (m/f)**	**dog**
mittere	to send	**veritas, veritatis**	**truth**
defendere	to defend	**virgo, virginis**	**virgin**
scribere	to write	**arbor, arboris (f)**	**tree**
sentire	to feel	**sol, solis (m)**	**sun**
munire	to build	**rex, regis (m)**	**king**
dicere	to say	**tempus, temporis (n)**	**time**
		civis, civis (m/f)	**citizen**

Make sure you memorize the following:

-o, or -m	I	-mus	we
-s	you (sing)	-tis	you
-t	he, she, or it	-nt	they

sum, es, est, sumus, estis, sunt *(I am, you are, he is, we are, you are, they are)*

eram, eras, erat, eramus, eratis, erant *(I was, you were, he was, we were, you were, they were)*

ero, eris, erit, erimus, eritis, erunt *(I will be, you will be, he will be, we will be, you will be, they will be)*

possum, potes, potest, possumus, potestis, possunt *(I am able, you are able, he is able, we are able, you are able, they are able)*

poteram, poteras, poterat, poteramus, poteratis, poterant *(I was able, you were able, he was able, we were able, you were able, they were able)*

potero, poteris, poterit, poterimus, poteritis, poterunt *(I will be able, you will be able, he will be able, we will be able, you will be able, they will be able)*

Remember your rules for gender:

Feminine nouns usually end in s-o-x

Neuter nouns usually end in l-a-n-c-e-t

Masculine nouns end in er-r-or

**Words that clearly denote a person of a particular gender are in that gender.
(Ex: Cicero is masculine)**

Day 1, Exercise 1: Give the gender of the following words. An "m" means "masculine," an "f" means feminine, and an "n" means "neuter."

The best way to do this is to first follow the rules, then check the vocabulary list to see if the word is an exception.

F   A. crux, crucis   *N*   B. flumen, fluminis

M   C. mons, montis   *M*   D. dolor, doloris

F   E. pax, pacis   *N*   F. caput, capitis

M   G. Cicero, Ciceronis   *F*   H. virgo, virginis

Day 1, Exercise 2: The subject form of a noun in Latin is called the nominative. The first form you are given is called the nominative form. Here are the nominative forms of a few of your words:

dolor, doloris	pain, sorrow
panis, panis	bread
mons, montis	mountain

Please underline the nominative of these words:

<u>urbs</u>, urbis	<u>flumen</u>, fluminis	<u>civitas</u>, civitatis
<u>pax</u>, pacis	<u>caput</u>, capitis	<u>Caesar</u>, Caesaris
<u>Cicero</u>, Ciceronis (m)	<u>canis</u>, canis (m/f)	<u>veritas</u>, veritatis
<u>virgo</u>, virginis	<u>arbor</u>, arboris (f)	<u>sol</u>, solis (m)

Day 2, Exercise 1: Synopsis the verb -credere.

I have a complete synopsis here for the verb "regere"

	Present	Past	Future
1st Singular	rego*	regebam	regam*
2nd Singular	regis	regebas	reges
3rd Singular	regit	regebat	reget
1st Plural	regimus	regebamus	regemus
2nd Plural	regitis	regebatis	regetis
3rd Plural	regunt*	regebant	regent

*These forms don't follow the regular rules. Memorize them.

(This exercise is continued on the next page.)

The gray shading is to remind you that these forms are the ones that are different and need to be memorized.

	Present	Past	Future
1st Singular	*credo*	*credebam*	*credam*
2nd Singular	*credis*	*credebas*	*credes*
3rd Singular	*credit*	*credebat*	*credet*
1st Plural	*credimus*	*credebamus*	*credemus*
2nd Plural	*creditis*	*credebatis*	*credetis*
3rd Plural	*credunt*	*credebant*	*credent*

In Latin, there are some very basic endings:

-o, or -m	I		-mus	we
-s	you (sing)		-tis	you
-t	he, she, or it		-nt	they

These endings give you a subject for your sentence. Sometimes, though, in the third person (t, nt) you can replace the third person ending with a noun. Here are some examples:

MODEL

"He believes" in Latin would be "Credit". "She believes" in Latin would also be "Credit". But you could replace the "he" or "she" with a name: "The man believes" which in Latin would be "Homo credit."

Now you translate: Peace lives.

(This exercise is continued on the next page.)

First thing you do is think "Peace/it lives." Now how do you say "it lives"?

"Live" is "vivere". You want the present (lives), third person singular (she). So, we take our stem: "vive" and add the "t" for "it" and change the "e" to "i". We now have "vivit". Add "peace" to that in the nominative form. The nominative form is the first form. So, "pax".

We have our sentence "pax vivit".

Day 2, Exercise 2: Now you translate.

Caesar conquers. <u>***Caesar vincit***</u>

The king rules. <u>***Rex regit***</u>

Day 3, Exercise 1: Translating step by step

Example:

1. The cross conquers.

Cross out "the", "a" or "an":	~~The~~ cross conquers
Give the vocabulary words:	crux, crucis vincere
Put a box around the verb word:	crux, crucis [vincere]
Figure out the pronoun that goes with "conquers":	it /it conquers
What ending do you use for the verb?	t
Get the stem of your verb:	vince
What tense is the verb?	present
What changes do you make to get the present (rule)?	Change "e" to "i"
What is the verb (take stem + apply rule + add ending)?	vincit
Which of the two forms is the nominative (subject) form?	crux
The sentence is:	Crux vincit.

(This exercise is continued on the next page.)

2. The man will believe.

Cross out "the", "a" or "an": ~~The~~ man will believe

Give the vocabulary words: **_homo, hominis   credere_**

Put a box around the verb word: **_homo, hominis_** |**_credere_**|

Figure out the pronoun that goes with 'will believe': **_he/he will believe_**

What ending do you use for the verb? **_t_**

Get the stem of your verb: **_crede_**

What tense is the verb? **_future_**

What changes do you make to get the future (give the rule? **_nothing (for future, you leave the stem the way it is)_**

What is the verb (take stem + apply rule + add ending)? **_credet_**

Which of the two forms is the nominative (subject) / first form of the noun? **_homo_**

The sentence is: **_Homo credet._**

3. A dog lives.

Cross out "the", "a" or "an": ~~A~~ dog lives.

Give the vocabulary words: **_canis, canis   vivere_**

Put a box around the verb word: **_canis, canis_** |**_vivere_**|

Figure out the pronoun that goes with 'lives': **_it/it lives_**

What ending do you use for the verb? **_t_**

Get the stem of your verb: **_vive_**

What tense is the verb? **_present_**

What changes do you make to get the present (give the rule? **_change "e" to "i"_**

What is the verb (take stem + apply rule + add ending)? **_vivit_**

Which of the two forms is the nominative (subject) / first form of the noun? **_canis_**

The sentence is: **_Canis vivit._**

So, nouns have two forms that you have learned. The first is the nominative form. What is the second? It is called the genitive form in Latin. In English we call it the possessive form. We use this genitive form to find the stem of our nouns, but we can also use it to express possession. So, in English we express possession like this: Mary's dog. In Latin you do it using the second form.

So, Caesar's city is *Caesaris urbs*.

Now you do some:

Day 3, Exercise 2: Translate.

1. Regis mons   *The king's mountain**

2. Civis panis   *The citizen's bread*

3. Ciceronis dolor   *Cicero's sorrow*

Remember, in English you may add "the," "a," or "an" to a sentence to make it sound right.

Lesson VII

Go over these every day for 5 minutes. New words are in bold.

laudare	to praise	mons, montis (m)	mountain
monēre	to warn	crux, crucis	cross
audire	to hear	homo, hominis (m)	man
agere	to act, to do	urbs, urbis	city
bibere	to drink	flumen, fluminis	river
edere	to eat	civitas, civitatis	state
vivere	to live	pax, pacis	peace
ponere	to put, to place	caput, capitis	head
regere	to rule	Caesar, Caesaris	Caesar
vincere	to conquer	Cicero, Ciceronis (m)	Cicero
credere	to believe	canis, canis (m/f)	dog
ducere	to lead	veritas, veritatis	truth
currere	to run	virgo, virginis	virgin
mittere	to send	arbor, arboris (f)	tree
defendere	to defend	sol, solis (m)	sun
scribere	to write	rex, regis (m)	king
sentire	to feel	tempus, temporis (n)	time
munire	to build	civis, civis (m/f)	citizen
dicere	to say	**dux, ducis (m)**	**leader**
dolor, doloris	pain, sorrow	**lux, lucis**	**light**
panis, panis (m)	bread	**lex, legis**	**law**

SPECIAL INDECLINABLE* WORDS:

non	not
diu	for a long time
saepe	often

* Indeclinable means they never change. They never change even an ending.

Make sure you memorize the following.

-o, or -m	I	-mus	we
-s	you (sing)	-tis	you
-t	he, she, or it	-nt	they

sum, es, est, sumus, estis, sunt *(I am, you are, he is, we are, you are, they are)*

eram, eras, erat, eramus, eratis, erant *(I was, you were, he was, we were, you were, they were)*

ero, eris, erit, erimus, eritis, erunt *(I will be, you will be, he will be, we will be, you will be, they will be)*

possum, potes, potest, possumus, potestis, possunt *(I am able, you are able, he is able, we are able, you are able, they are able)*

poteram, poteras, poterat, poteramus, poteratis, poterant *(I was able, you were able, he was able, we were able, you were able, they were able)*

potero, poteris, poterit, poterimus, poteritis, poterunt *(I will be able, you will be able, he will be able, we will be able, you will be able, they will be able)*

Remember your rules for gender:

Feminine nouns usually end in s-o-x

Neuter nouns usually end in l-a-n-c-e-t

Masculine nouns end in er-r-or

Words that clearly denote a person of a particular gender are in that gender.
(Ex: Cicero is masculine)

Day 1, Exercise 1: Underline the endings in the following words:

m,o	s	t	mus	tis	nt
su**m**	e**s**	es**t**	su**mus**	es**tis**	su**nt**
era**m**	era**s**	era**t**	era**mus**	era**tis**	era**nt**
er**o**	eri**s**	eri**t**	eri**mus**	eri**tis**	eru**nt**

Day 1, Exercise 2: Translating step by step

Example: The king's cross conquers.

Cross out "the", "a" or "an":	~~The~~ cross conquers
Give the vocabulary words:	crux, crucis vincere
Put a box around the verb word:	crux, crucis [vincere]
Figure out the pronoun that goes with conquers:	it /it conquers
What ending do you use for the verb?	t
Get the stem of your verb:	vince
What tense is the sentence?	present
What changes do you make to get the present (rule)?	change "e" to "i"
What is the verb (take stem + apply rule + add ending)?	vincit
Which of the two forms (crux, crucis) is the nominative (subject) form? crux	
Which of the two forms (rex, regis) is the genitive (possessive) form? regis	
The sentence is:	Regis crux vincit.

(This exercise is continued on the next page.)

1. <u>A man's dog eats.</u>

Cross out "the", "a" or "an".   **A~~ ~~man's dog eats.**

Give the vocabulary words: 1. **homo, hominis**   2. **canis, canis**   3. **edere**

Put a box around the verb word.   **☐edere☐**

Figure out the pronoun (he, she, it, I, you) that goes with eats: **it/it eats**

What ending do you use for the verb?   **t**

Get the stem of your verb: **ede**

What tense is the sentence?   **present**

What changes do you make to get the present (give the rule)?   **change "e" to "i"**

What is the verb (take stem + apply rule + add ending)?   **edit**

Which of the two forms of "dog" is the nominative form?   **canis**

Which of the two forms of "man" is the genitive form?   **hominis**

The sentence is: **Hominis canis edit.**

2. <u>The city's citizen was acting.</u>

Cross out "the", "a" or "an".   **~~The~~ city's citizen was acting.**

Give the vocabulary words: 1. **urbs, urbis**   2. **civis, civis**   3. **agere**

Put a box around the verb word.   **☐agere☐**

Figure out the pronoun (he, she, it, I, you) that goes with "was acting":   **he/he was acting**

What ending do you use for the verb?   **t**

Get the stem of your verb: **age**

What tense is the sentence?   **past**

What changes do you make to get the past (give the rule)?   **add "ba" to the stem**

(This exercise is continued on the next page.)

What is the verb (take stem + apply rule + add ending)?	*agebat*
Which of the two forms of "citizen" is the nominative form?	*civis*
Which of the two forms of "city" is the genitive form?	*urbis*
The sentence is:	**Urbis civis agebat.**

Day 2, Exercise 1: Remember that you have been doing a synopsis of your verbs. Now you should do a synopsis of "defendere". The gray shading is to remind you that these forms are the ones that are different and need to be memorized.

	Present	Past	Future
1st Singular	*defendo*	*defendebam*	*defendam*
2nd Singular	*defendis*	*defendebas*	*defendes*
3rd Singular	*defendit*	*defendebat*	*defendet*
1st Plural	*defendimus*	*defendebamus*	*defendemus*
2nd Plural	*defenditis*	*defendebatis*	*defendetis*
3rd Plural	*defendunt*	*defendebant*	*defendent*

Remember that so far with verbs we have been dealing with words that end in "ere", right? Well, now we will start with verbs that end in "ire". These are fourth conjugation verbs. You know one: "audire". We will look at that verb this week. The first thing to know is that its stem is "audi". So look at the present below. It doesn't have to change the "e" to "i". It is already done!

Compare "audire" to good old "regere":

3rd Present	4th Present	3rd Past	4th Past
rego	audio	regebam	audiebam
regis	audis	regebas	audiebas
regit	audit	regebat	audiebat
regimus	audimus	regebamus	audiebamus
regitis	auditis	regebatis	audiebatis
regunt	audiunt	regebant	audiebant

3rd Future	4th Future
regam	audiam
reges	audies
reget	audiet
regemus	audiemus
regetis	audietis
regent	audient

It seems the new word loves its "i"! It doesn't get rid of it. It doesn't have to change the "e" to "i" for the present, because it is already an "i". It adds the "e" for the past and future, so it can be just like the third conjugation -ere words, but it doesn't lose its "i". It loves its "i".

Day 2, Exercise 2: Remember that you have been doing a synopsis of your verbs. Now you should do a synopsis of "audire". The gray shading is to remind you that these forms are the ones that are different and need to be memorized.

	Present	Past	Future
1st Singular	audio	audiebam	audiam
2nd Singular	audis	audiebas	audies
3rd Singular	audit	audiebat	audiet
1st Plural	audimus	audiebamus	audiemus
2nd Plural	auditis	audiebatis	audietis
3rd Plural	audiunt	audiebant	audient

NOUNS

So far you know the nominative (subject) and the possessive (genitive) form of nouns. Today we will review the accusative (direct object) form. It is what receives the <u>action of the verb performed by a subject.</u>

<u>Mary calls the dog.</u>   In this sentence, "dog" is the direct object. It receives the action of calling performed by Mary.

Here's how you can figure this out.

1. Find the action word: calls

2. Ask yourself: Who/What calls? Answer: Mary   This is the subject.

3. Mary calls whom/what? Answer: dog   This is the direct object.

Day 3, Exercise 1: Underline the direct objects in these sentences. Before you do this, answer questions 1-3, below each sentence.

A. Mary calls <u>Joseph</u>.

1. Find the action word (also known as the verb):   *__calls__*

2. Who/What calls? *__Mary__*   This is the subject.

3. Mary calls whom/what? *__Joseph__*   This is the direct object. Underline it.

B. The chicken ate <u>corn</u>.

1. Find the action word (also known as the verb): *__ate__*

2. Who/What ate? *__chicken__*   This is the subject.

3. Chicken ate whom/what? *__corn__*   This is the direct object. Underline it.

C. The children helped the <u>lady</u>.

1. Find the action word (also known as the verb):   *__helped__*

2. Who/What helped? *__the children__*   This is the subject.

3. Children helped whom/what? *__the lady__* This is the direct object. Underline it.

Subjects are nominative in Latin.

Possessives are genitive in Latin.

Direct objects are accusative in Latin.

In Latin you have learned that the first form of the noun is the subject or nominative form and the second form is the possessive or genitive form. So, for example, with "sol, solis", the subject form is "sol" and the possessive form is "solis". Now, what's the direct object or accusative form?

Well you have to make it by dropping the "is" on the end of the possessive form to get the stem, and then add "em".

arboris
- is

arbor
+ em
arborem

You practice.

Day 3, Exercise 2: Give me the accusative for the following words:

canis, canis	*canem*
virgo, virginis	*virginem*
civitas, civitatis	*civitatem*
mons, montis	*montem*
lux, lucis	*lucem*

Lesson VIII
Go over these every day for 10 minutes.

laudare	to praise	mons, montis (m)	mountain
monēre	to warn	crux, crucis	cross
audire	to hear	homo, hominis (m)	man
agere	to act, to do	urbs, urbis	city
bibere	to drink	flumen, fluminis	river
edere	to eat	civitas, civitatis	state
vivere	to live	pax, pacis	peace
ponere	to put, to place	caput, capitis	head
regere	to rule	Caesar, Caesaris	Caesar
vincere	to conquer	Cicero, Ciceronis (m)	Cicero
credere	to believe	canis, canis (m/f)	dog
ducere	to lead	veritas, veritatis	truth
currere	to run	virgo, virginis	virgin
mittere	to send	arbor, arboris (f)	tree
defendere	to defend	sol, solis (m)	sun
scribere	to write	rex, regis (m)	king
sentire	to feel	tempus, temporis (n)	time
munire	to build	civis, civis (m/f)	citizen
dicere	to say	dux, ducis (m)	leader
dolor, doloris	pain, sorrow	lux, lucis	light
panis, panis (m)	bread	lex, legis	law

SPECIAL INDECLINABLE* WORDS:

non	not
diu	for a long time
saepe	often

Indeclinable means they never change. They never change even an ending.

Make sure you memorize the following.

-o, or -m	I	-mus	we
-s	you (sing)	-tis	you
-t	he, she, or it	-nt	they

sum, es, est, sumus, estis, sunt *(I am, you are, he is, we are, you are, they are)*

eram, eras, erat, eramus, eratis, erant *(I was, you were, he was, we were, you were, they were)*

ero, eris, erit, erimus, eritis, erunt *(I will be, you will be, he will be, we will be, you will be, they will be)*

possum, potes, potest, possumus, potestis, possunt *(I am able, you are able, he is able, we are able, you are able, they are able)*

poteram, poteras, poterat, poteramus, poteratis, poterant *(I was able, you were able, he was able, we were able, you were able, they were able)*

potero, poteris, poterit, poterimus, poteritis, poterunt *(I will be able, you will be able, he will be able, we will be able, you will be able, they will be able)*

volo, vis, vult, volumus, vultis, volunt *(I am willing, you are willing, he is willing, we are willing, you are willing, they are willing)* *

*Just memorize this word and its meanings for now.

Remember your rules for gender:

> **Feminine nouns usually end in s-o-x**
>
> **Neuter nouns usually end in l-a-n-c-e-t**
>
> **Masculine nouns end in er-r-or**
>
> **Words that clearly denote a person of a particular gender are in that gender.**
> **(Ex: Cicero is masculine)**

Day 1, Exercise 1: With each of the following words underline its case in Latin.

Example: veritas   <u>nominative</u>   accusative   genitive

Remember the first form of the noun is the nominative, the second form of the noun is the genitive, and the accusative is the stem + em.

1. arboris   nominative   accusative   ***<u>genitive</u>***

2. virginem   nominative   ***<u>accusative</u>***   genitive

3. crucem   nominative   ***<u>accusative</u>***   genitive

4. doloris   nominative   accusative   ***<u>genitive</u>***

5. virgo   ***<u>nominative</u>***   accusative   genitive

6. homo   ***<u>nominative</u>***   accusative   genitive

Day 1, Exercise 2: Give the stem of the following words.

1. laudare	*lauda*	2. agere	*age*
3. regere	*rege*	4. urbs, urbis	*urb*
5. mittere	*mitte*	6. canis, canis	*can*
7. flumen, fluminis	*flumin*	8. pax, pacis	*pac*

Study the -ire verb "audire" below. The first thing to know is that its stem is "audi". So look at the present below. It doesn't have to change the "e" to "i". It is already done!

Compare "audire" to good old "regere":

3rd Present	4th Present	3rd Past	4th Past
rego	audio	regebam	audiebam
regis	audis	regebas	audiebas
regit	audit	regebat	audiebat
regimus	audimus	regebamus	audiebamus
regitis	auditis	regebatis	audiebatis
regunt	audiunt	regebant	audiebant

3rd Future	4th Future
regam	audiam
reges	audies
reget	audiet
regemus	audiemus
regetis	audietis
regent	audient

A verb that loves its i will keep it, but otherwise it copycats the -ere verbs. It doesn't have to change the "e" to "i" for the present, because it is already an "i". However, it adds the "e" for the past and future, so it can be just like the third conjugation -ere words, but it doesn't lose its "i". It loves its "i".

Day 2, Exercise 1: Remember that you have been doing a synopsis of your verbs. Now you should do a synopsis of "munire". The gray shading is to remind you that these forms are the ones that are different and need to be memorized.

	Present	Past	Future
1st Singular	*munio*	*muniebam*	*muniam*
2nd Singular	*munis*	*muniebas*	*munies*
3rd Singular	*munit*	*muniebat*	*muniet*
1st Plural	*munimus*	*muniebamus*	*muniemus*
2nd Plural	*munitis*	*muniebatis*	*munietis*
3rd Plural	*muniunt*	*muniebant*	*munient*

Expressing possibility in Latin

Remember when I originally defined the future tense as expressing something that will happen in the future or is possible? Well if you think about it, those are really two different kinds of futures. Something that will happen is a fact. "The sun will rise in the morning." This is true, even though it is in the future. When you ask something like, "May I have some cake?" You hope the answer is "yes" but you aren't sure your mom will say "yes." You wouldn't ask, of course, if there was no possibility of having cake, but if there is a cake in the house, then you ask and you hope she says "yes." So, we are going to come up with a new form for the possible. Here it is:

3rd Possibles	4th Possibles
regam	audiam
regas	audias
regat	audiat
regamus	audiamus
regatis	audiatis
regant	audiant

Instead of using "will" or "shall" with these, use "may" or "let".

So, regular future is: He will eat cake.

Possibility is: He may eat cake. May he eat cake. May he eat cake? Let him eat cake!

Day 2, Exercise 2: Now compare possibility to regular futures. What is the difference? Make a rule for this.

In possibility, you change the "e" on the stem to an "a" and add the ending, whereas in regular futures, you keep the stem and just add the ending (except the first person singular exception).

Today we will be working on complex translations.

Day 3, Exercise 1: Translate, following these steps.

Step 1: Please circle the subject, box the possessives and underline the direct objects. Cross out the words, "the," "a," or "an."

Step 2: Write the Latin word you would use on line A above the word. Remember that there is no Latin word for "the," "a," or "an."

Step 3: Write the stem of the words (which need the stem form) on line B.

Step 4: Add the correct endings to complete the translation on line C.

Now let's apply these steps to the first sentence below:

The man will defend Caesar.

Step 1: Please circle the subject, box the possessives and underline the direct objects. Cross out the words, "the," "a," or "an."

a) Locate the verb. It has a shaded box below it. So in this sentence it is "will defend".

b) Ask yourself "Who/what will defend?" Answer: Man. "Man" is the subject; circle it.

c) The man will defend whom/what? Answer: Caesar. "Caesar" is the direct object; underline it.

d) Are there any possessives? These words have 's in them. In this sentence, there are none.

e) Cross out any "the", "a", or "an"s. So, cross out the word "the" in this sentence.

(This exercise is continued on the next page.)

50

> Step 2: Write the Latin word you would use on line A above the word. Remember that there is no Latin word for "the," "a," or "an."

On line "A", write the words as they appear in your vocabulary. Put "NA" for any words that are not translated. So, you would have:

The = NA (line A)

man = homo, hominis (line A)

will defend = defendere (line A)

Caesar = Caesar, Caesaris (line A)

> Step 3: Write the stem of the words (which need the stem form) on line B.

You only have to write the stem for words that need the stem to build the word. So, in this case put the stem down for defendere (defende) and Caesar, Caesaris (Caesar).

> Step 4: Add the correct endings to complete the translation on line C.

The correct form of "homo, hominis" is the first form, which is the nominative form used for the subject. So it is **homo**.

The correct form of "Caesar, Caesaris" is the stem + em, which is the accusative form used for the direct object. So it is **Caesarem.**

The shaded box reminds you this is a verb word so think about these things when you translate that word.

a) What is the tense? **Answer: future.**

b) What do you do to the stem because of that tense? For example, change e to i to get the present for an -ere word.) **Answer: Leave it alone.**

c) What personal ending do you use? (In other words: is "man" an "I" , "you", "he", "she", or "it"?) Plug in your word in the shaded box. **Answer: "t" for "he". Word is "defendet."**

(This exercise is continued on the next page.)

1.

A. <u>**NA**</u>   <u>**homo, hominis**</u>   <u>**credere**</u>   <u>**Caesar, Caesaris**</u>

B.   <u>**crede**</u>   <u>**Caesar**</u>

~~The~~   (man)   will believe   Caesar.

C.   <u>**Homo**</u>   <u>**credet**</u>   <u>**Caesarem.**</u>

2.

A. <u>**NA**</u>   <u>**munire**</u>   <u>**NA**</u>   <u>**urbs, urbis**</u>

B.   <u>**muni**</u>   <u>**urb**</u>

He   was building   ~~the~~   city.

C.   * <u>**Muniebat**</u>   <u>**urbem.**</u>

* Munire is an i-lover. Remember i-lovers keep their "i" always. They also copycat the -ere verbs. Look at Day 2, Exercise 3.

3.

A. <u>**NA**</u> <u>**homo, hominis**</u> <u>**canis, canis**</u>   <u>**defendere**</u>   <u>**Cicero, Ciceronis**</u>

B.   <u>**defende**</u>   <u>**Ciceron**</u>

~~A~~   [man's]   (dog)   defends   Cicero.

C.   <u>**Hominis**</u>   <u>**canis**</u>   <u>**defendit**</u>   <u>**Ciceronem**</u>

Day 3, Exercise 2: True or False

_F_   We use the accusative case for subjects in Latin.

_T_   With -ere verbs, if you want to make a present, you need to change the "e" of the stem to "i".

_F_   When you add "ba" to the stem you have a future tense.

_T_   We use the nominative case for subjects in Latin.

_T_   Genitives in Latin are called possessives in English.

Review Lesson A

Day 1, Exercise 1: Do a complete synopsis of the verb "agere".

	Present	Past	Future Regulars	Future Possibles
1st Singular	*ago*	*agebam*	*agam*	*agam*
2nd Singular	*agis*	*agebas*	*ages*	*agas*
3rd Singular	*agit*	*agebat*	*aget*	*agat*
1st Plural	*agimus*	*agebamus*	*agemus*	*agamus*
2nd Plural	*agitis*	*agebatis*	*agetis*	*agatis*
3rd Plural	*agunt*	*agebant*	*agent*	*agant*

Day 1, Exercise 2: True or False

laudare.................................to warn	True	***False***
monēre.................................to praise	True	***False***
audire..................................to hear	***True***	False
agere...................................to do	***True***	False
civitas, civitatis...................state	***True***	False
pax, pacis............................peace	***True***	False
caput, capitis.......................cross	True	***False***
Caesar, Caesaris..................Caesar	***True***	False
diu.......................................for a long time	***True***	False
lux, lucis.............................law	True	***False***

Day 1, Exercise 3: Fill in the blanks.

	Word	Meaning
1st Singular	*possum*	I am able
2nd Singular	*potes*	you are able
3rd Singular	*potest*	he is able
1st Plural	*possumus*	we are able
2nd Plural	*potestis*	you are able
3rd Plural	*possunt*	they are able

	Word	Meaning
1st Singular	*sum*	I am
2nd Singular	*es*	you are
3rd Singular	*est*	he is
1st Plural	*sumus*	we are
2nd Plural	*estis*	you are
3rd Plural	*sunt*	they are

Day 1, Exercise 4: Find the stem of the following words.

scribere *scribe*   mittere *mitte*

lux, lucis *luc*   vivere *vive*

flumen, fluminis *flumin* caput, capitis *capit*

arbor, arboris *arbor*   panis, panis *pan*

Day 2, Exercise 1: True or False

bibere..to drink	***True***	False
edere..to edit	True	***False***
vivere..to conquer	True	***False***
ponere...to place	***True***	False
regere..to rule	***True***	False
non..for a long time	True	***False***
urbs, urbis...herb	True	***False***
flumen, fluminis...................................river	***True***	False
Cicero, Ciceronis (m)...........................Cicero	***True***	False
canis, canis (m/f..................................dog	***True***	False
veritas, veritatis....................................virgin	True	***False***
virgo, virginis.......................................virgin	***True***	False

Day 2, Exercise 2: Do a complete synopsis of the verb "audire".

	Present	Past	Future Regulars	Future Possibles
1st Singular	*audio*	*audiebam*	*audiam*	*audiam*
2nd Singular	*audis*	*audiebas*	*audies*	*audias*
3rd Singular	*audit*	*audiebat*	*audiet*	*audiat*
1st Plural	*audimus*	*audiebamus*	*audiemus*	*audiamus*
2nd Plural	*auditis*	*audiebatis*	*audietis*	*audiatis*
3rd Plural	*audiunt*	*audiebant*	*audient*	*audiant*

Day 2, Exercise 3: Match the correct associations.

Subject *(Nominative)*	L-A-N-C-E-T
Possessive *(Genitive)*	ER-R-OR
3rd Person Plural *(They)*	Genitive
Feminine Words *(S-O-X)*	He, She, It
3rd Person Singular *(He, She, It)*	Accusative
Neuter Words *(L-A-N-C-E-T)*	You (sing)
2nd Person Singular *(You (sing))*	S-O-X
1st Person Singular *(I)*	They
Direct Objects *(Accusative)*	Nominative
Masculine Words *(ER-R-OR)*	We
1st Person Plural *(We)*	I

Day 2, Exercise 4: Fill in the blanks.

	Word	Meaning
1st Singular	poteram	*I was able*
2nd Singular	poteras	*you were able*
3rd Singular	poterat	*he was able*
1st Plural	poteramus	*we were able*
2nd Plural	poteratis	*you were able*
3rd Plural	poterant	*they were able*

(This exercise is continued on the next page.)

	Word	**Meaning**
1st Singular	*eram*	I was
2nd Singular	*eras*	you were
3rd Singular	*erat*	she was
1st Plural	*eramus*	we were
2nd Plural	*eratis*	you were
3rd Plural	*erant*	they were

Day 3, Exercise 1: True or False

vincere...to conquer   ***True***   False

credere..to believe   ***True***   False

ducere...to rule   True   ***False***

currere..to run   ***True***   False

mittere..to eat   True   ***False***

tempus, temporis (n).............................time   ***True***   False

civis, civis (m/f)......................................state   True   ***False***

dux, ducis (m)...leader   ***True***   False

lex, legis..light   True   ***False***

saepe..often   ***True***   False

Day 3, Exercise 2: Match.

Future Tense Regular *(I will call)*   I call.

Future Tense Possible *(May I call)*   I will call.

Present Tense *(I call)*   I was calling.

Past Tense *(I was calling)*   May I call.

Day 3, Exercise 3: Rules.

The -ire verbs love their *i's*. They also copycat the -ere verbs.

For the present tense, for -ere verbs, you change the "e" of the stem to *i*.

For the future tense regular, for -ere verbs, you *leave the stem alone*.

For the future tense possible, for -ere verbs, you *change the "e" to "a."*

For the past tense, for -ere verbs, you add *ba* to the stem, and then add the ending.

Day 3, Exercise 4: Fill in the blanks.

	Word	Meaning
1st Singular	ero	*I will be*
2nd Singular	eris	*you will be*
3rd Singular	erit	*he will be*
1st Plural	erimus	*we will be*
2nd Plural	eritis	*you will be*
3rd Plural	erunt	*they will be*

(This exercise is continued on the next page.)

	Word	Meaning
1st Singular	*potero*	I will be able
2nd Singular	*poteris*	you will be able
3rd Singular	*poterit*	it will be able
1st Plural	*poterimus*	we will be able
2nd Plural	*poteritis*	you will be able
3rd Plural	*poterunt*	they will be able

Day 3, Exercise 5: True or False

defendere..to conquer	True	***False***
scribere..to write	***True***	False
sentire...to rule	True	***False***
munire...to build	***True***	False
dicere..to speak	***True***	False
rex, regis (m)..king	***True***	False
crux, crucis...cross	***True***	False
dolor, doloris..sorrow	***True***	False
panis, panis (m)...peace	True	***False***
mons, montis (m).......................................mountain	***True***	False
homo, hominis (m)....................................man	***True***	False
arbor, arboris (f).......................................flower	True	***False***
sol, solis (m)...summit	True	***False***

Day 3, Exercise 6: For each of the following words, underline its case in Latin.

1. arborem   nominative   ***accusative***   genitive
2. dolor   ***nominative***   accusative   genitive
3. doloris   nominative   accusative   ***genitive***
4. hominis   nominative   accusative   ***genitive***
5. montem   nominative   ***accusative***   genitive

Lesson IX

Go over these every day for 10 minutes.

laudare	to praise	urbs, urbis	city
monēre	to warn	flumen, fluminis	river
audire	to hear	civitas, civitatis	state
agere	to act, to do	pax, pacis	peace
bibere	to drink	caput, capitis	head
edere	to eat	Caesar, Caesaris	Caesar
vivere	to live	Cicero, Ciceronis (m)	Cicero
ponere	to put, to place	canis, canis (m/f)	dog
regere	to rule	veritas, veritatis	truth
vincere	to conquer	virgo, virginis	virgin
credere	to believe	arbor, arboris (f)	tree
ducere	to lead	sol, solis (m)	sun
currere	to run	rex, regis (m)	king
mittere	to send	tempus, temporis (n)	time
defendere	to defend	civis, civis (m/f)	citizen
scribere	to write	dux, ducis (m)	leader
sentire	to feel	lux, lucis	light
munire	to build	lex, legis	law
dicere	to say	**gens, gentis**	**tribe**
dolor, doloris	pain, sorrow	**fons, fontis (m)**	**fountain**
panis, panis (m)	bread	**tentatio, tentationis**	**temptation**
mons, montis (m)	mountain	**caritas, caritatis**	**love**
crux, crucis	cross	**libertas, libertatis**	**freedom, liberty**
homo, hominis (m)	man	**pastor, pastoris**	**shepherd**

SPECIAL INDECLINABLE* WORDS:

non	not
diu	for a long time
saepe	often

* Indeclinable means they never change. They never change even an ending.

-o, or -m	I	-mus	we
-s	you (sing)	-tis	you
-t	he, she, or it	-nt	they

sum, es, est, sumus, estis, sunt *(I am, you are, he is, we are, you are, they are)*

eram, eras, erat, eramus, eratis, erant *(I was, you were, he was, we were, you were, they were)*

ero, eris, erit, erimus, eritis, erunt *(I will be, you will be, he will be, we will be, you will be, they will be)*

possum, potes, potest, possumus, potestis, possunt *(I am able, you are able, he is able, we are able, you are able, they are able)*

poteram, poteras, poterat, poteramus, poteratis, poterant *(I was able, you were able, he was able, we were able, you were able, they were able)*

potero, poteris, poterit, poterimus, poteritis, poterunt *(I will be able, you will be able, he will be able, we will be able, you will be able, they will be able)*

volo, vis, vult, volumus, vultis, volunt *(I am willing, you are willing, he is willing, we are willing, you are willing, they are willing)*

nolo, non vis, non vult, nolumus, non vultis, nolunt *(I am not willing, you are not willing, he is not willing, we are not willing, you are not willing, they are not willing)*

Remember your rules for gender:

Feminine nouns usually end in s-o-x
Neuter nouns usually end in l-a-n-c-e-t
Masculine nouns end in er-r-or
Words that clearly denote a person of a particular gender are in that gender.
(Ex: Cicero is masculine)

Remember the Latin names for English cases and how to get them:

> **Nominative = Subject = First Form**
>
> **Genitive = Possessive = Second Form**
>
> **Accusative = Direct Object = Stem + em**

There are special words called prepositions. Here are some of these words:

into	to	across	through	towards	against
before	after	by	with	from	out of
in	on	of	for		

Prepositions relate a noun to another word, like a noun or verb. They are always followed by a noun — that is, by a word that is a person, place, or thing. Let's look at an example:

The fish swims **in the water**.	Explanation: "in" is the preposition. "Water" is the word that follows it (because "the" doesn't really count, does it?) We call "water" the object of the preposition.
John hit the ball **into the water**.	Explanation: "into" is the preposition. "Water" is the word that follows it (because "the" doesn't really count, does it?) We call "water" the object of the preposition.

Beginning Latin II - Lesson IX

Day 1, Exercise 1: Circle the prepositions in the following sentences:

1. The cake is **_(on)_** the table.
2. The cat swam **_(against)_** the water.
3. **_(For)_** whom does the bell toll?
4. I went **_(through)_** the forest.
5. I got a letter **_(from)_** Lena.
6. I looked **_(across)_** the meadow.
8. 7. You should start **_(after)_** me.
Finish this **_(before)_** tomorrow.

Day 1, Exercise 2: Do a complete synopsis of the verb "mittere". The following chart will help.

3rd Present	4th Present	3rd Past	4th Past
rego	audio	regebam	audiebam
regis	audis	regebas	audiebas
regit	audit	regebat	audiebat
regimus	audimus	regebamus	audiebamus
regitis	auditis	regebatis	audiebatis
regunt	audiunt	regebant	audiebant

3rd Future Regular	4th Future Regular	3rd Future Possibles	4th Future Possibles
regam	audiam	regam	audiam
reges	audies	regas	audias
reget	audiet	regat	audiat
regemus	audiemus	regamus	audiamus
regetis	audietis	regatis	audiatis
regent	audient	regant	audiant

(This exercise is continued on the next page.)

A verb that loves its i will keep it, but otherwise it copycats the -ere verbs. It doesn't have to change the "e" to "i" for the present, because it is already an "i". However, it adds the "e" for the past and future, so it can be just like the third conjugation -ere words, but it doesn't lose its "i". It loves its "i".

	Present	Past	Future Regulars	Future Possibles
1st Singular	*mitto*	*mittebam*	*mittam*	*mittam*
2nd Singular	*mittis*	*mittebas*	*mittes*	*mittas*
3rd Singular	*mittit*	*mittebat*	*mittet*	*mittat*
1st Plural	*mittimus*	*mittebamus*	*mittemus*	*mittamus*
2nd Plural	*mittitis*	*mittebatis*	*mittetis*	*mittatis*
3rd Plural	*mittunt*	*mittebant*	*mittent*	*mittant*

We will begin to memorize the common prepositions in Latin.

in	in, on	ante	before
in	into, onto	post	after
ad	to, towards	a, ab	by
trans	across	cum	with
per	through	de	from
contra	against	e, ex	out of

(Continued on the next page.)

Prepositions relate a noun to another word, like a noun or verb. They are always followed by a noun — that is by a word that is a person, place, or thing. Let's look at an example:

The fish swims **in** the water.

Explanation: "in" is the preposition. "Water" is the word that follows it (because "the" doesn't really count, does it?) We call "water" the object of the preposition.

John hit the ball **into** the water.

Explanation: "into" is the preposition. "Water" is the word that follows it (because "the" doesn't really count, does it?) We call "water" the object of the preposition.

Day 2, Exercise 3: Underline the object of the prepositions in the following sentences:

1. The book is on the **desk**.

2. The kite sailed in the **wind**.

3. I want to go out for *ice cream*.

4. I went into the **forest**.

5. I got here before my **sister**.

6. I ran across the **stream**.

7. You should start after **Mary**.

8. Finish this before **tomorrow**.

Day 2, Exercise 4: Answer the questions:

1. Which 2 prepositions from your list yesterday did I not give you the meaning of in Latin today? (Hint: the English prepositions both have an "o" and an "f" in them!)

"of" and "for"

(This exercise is continued on the next page.)

2. Is "to" a preposition? <u>*yes*</u>

3. What is another way, other than "ad" to say "to" in Latin? <u>***"re" on the end of a verb makes it say "to"***</u>

(Hint: Look at your vocabulary list at the start of this lesson. Do you notice that all the verbs end in "re" and all the verbs, in English, start with "to". Does that help you?)

Day 3, Exercise 1: Fill in the charts:

	Word	Meaning
1st Singular	*volo*	I am willing
2nd Singular	*vis*	you are willing
3rd Singular	*vult*	he is willing
1st Plural	*volumus*	we are willing
2nd Plural	*vultis*	you are willing
3rd Plural	*volunt*	they are willing

	Word	Meaning
1st Singular	*nolo*	I am not willing
2nd Singular	*non vis*	you are not willing
3rd Singular	*non vult*	he is not willing
1st Plural	*nolumus*	we are not willing
2nd Plural	*non vultis*	you are not willing
3rd Plural	*nolunt*	they are not willing

Day 3, Exercise 2: Translate, following these steps.

Step 1: Please circle the subject, box the possessives and underline the direct objects. Cross out the words, "the," "a," or "an."

Step 2: Write the Latin word you would use on line A above the word. Remember that there is no Latin word for "the," "a," or "an."

Step 3: Write the stem of the words (which need the stem form) on line B.

Step 4: Add the correct endings to complete the translation on line C.

Now let's apply these steps to this example: *The man will believe Caesar.*

Step 1: Please circle the subject, box the possessives and underline the direct objects. Cross out the words, "the," "a," or "an."

a) Locate the verb. It has a shaded box below it. So in this sentence it is "will believe".

b) Ask yourself "Who/what will believe?" Answer: Man. "Man" is the subject; circle it.

c) The man will believe whom/what? Answer: Caesar. "Caesar" is the direct object; underline it.

d) Are there any possessives? These words have 's in them. In this sentence, there are none.

e) Cross out any "the", "a", or "an"s. So, cross out the word "the" in this sentence.

Step 2: Write the Latin word you would use on line A above the word. Remember that there is no Latin word for "the," "a," or "an."

(This exercise is continued on the next page.)

On line "A", write the words as they appear in your vocabulary. Put "NA" for any words that are not translated. So, you would have:

The = NA (line A)

man = homo, hominis (line A)

will believe = credere (line A)

Caesar = Caesar, Caesaris (line A)

Step 3: Write the stem of the words (which need the stem form) on line B.

You only have to write the stem for words that need the stem to build the word. So, in this case put the stem down for credere (crede) and Caesar, Caesaris (Caesar).

Step 4: Add the correct endings to complete the translation on line C.

The correct form of "homo, hominis" is the first form, which is the nominative form used for the subject. So it is **homo**.

The correct form of "Caesar, Caesaris" is the stem + em, which is the accusative form used for the direct object. So it is **Caesarem.**

The shaded box reminds you this is a verb word so think about these things when you translate that word.

a) What is the tense? **Answer: future.**

b) What do you do to the stem because of that tense? For example, change e to i to get the present for an -ere word.) Answer: Leave it alone.

c) What personal ending do you use? (In other words is "man" an "I," "you," "he," "she," or "it.") Plug in your word in the shaded box. **Answer: "t" for "he". Word is "credet."**

(This exercise is continued on the next page.)

1.

A. _NA_ _pastor, pastoris_ _defendere_ _NA_ _canis, canis_

B. _defende_ _can_

~~A~~ (shepherd) was defending ~~the~~ dog.

C. **_Pastor_** _defendebat_ _canem_

2.

A. NA _audire_ NA _veritas, veritatis_

B. _audi_ _veritat_

(He) hears* ~~the~~ truth.

C. _audit_ _veritatem_

* Remember i-lovers keep their "i" always. They also copycat the -ere verbs.

3.

A. _Caesar, Caesaris_ _urbs, urbis_ _vincere_ _NA_ _gens, gentis_

B. _Caesar_ _vince_ _gent_

Caesar's (city) conquers ~~the~~ tribe.

C. _Caesaris_ _urbs_ _vincit_ _gentem_

Lesson X

Go over these every day for 10 minutes.

laudare	to praise	urbs, urbis	city
monēre	to warn	flumen, fluminis	river
audire	to hear	civitas, civitatis	state
agere	to act, to do	pax, pacis	peace
bibere	to drink	caput, capitis	head
edere	to eat	Caesar, Caesaris	Caesar
vivere	to live	Cicero, Ciceronis (m)	Cicero
ponere	to put, to place	canis, canis (m/f)	dog
regere	to rule	veritas, veritatis	truth
vincere	to conquer	virgo, virginis	virgin
credere	to believe	arbor, arboris (f)	tree
ducere	to lead	sol, solis (m)	sun
currere	to run	rex, regis (m)	king
mittere	to send	tempus, temporis (n)	time
defendere	to defend	civis, civis (m/f)	citizen
scribere	to write	dux, ducis (m)	leader
sentire	to feel	lux, lucis	light
munire	to build	lex, legis	law
dicere	to say	gens, gentis	tribe
dolor, doloris	pain, sorrow	fons, fontis (m)	fountain
panis, panis (m)	bread	tentatio, tentationis	temptation
mons, montis (m)	mountain	caritas, caritatis	love
crux, crucis	cross	libertas, libertatis	freedom, liberty
homo, hominis (m)	man	pastor, pastoris	shepherd

SPECIAL INDECLINABLE* WORDS:

non	not	contra	against
diu	for a long time	ante	before
saepe	often	post	after
in	in, on	a, ab	by
in	into, onto	cum	with
ad	to, towards	de	from
trans	across	e, ex	out of
per	through		

* *Indeclinable means they never change. They never change even an ending.*

-o, or -m	I	-mus	we
-s	you (sing)	-tis	you
-t	he, she, or it	-nt	they

sum, es, est, sumus, estis, sunt *(I am, you are, he is, we are, you are, they are)*

eram, eras, erat, eramus, eratis, erant *(I was, you were, he was, we were, you were, they were)*

ero, eris, erit, erimus, eritis, erunt *(I will be, you will be, he will be, we will be, you will be, they will be)*

possum, potes, potest, possumus, potestis, possunt *(I am able, you are able, he is able, we are able, you are able, they are able)*

poteram, poteras, poterat, poteramus, poteratis, poterant *(I was able, you were able, he was able, we were able, you were able, they were able)*

potero, poteris, poterit, poterimus, poteritis, poterunt *(I will be able, you will be able, he will be able, we will be able, you will be able, they will be able)*

volo, vis, vult, volumus, vultis, volunt *(I am willing, you are willing, he is willing, we are willing, you are willing, they are willing)*

nolo, non vis, non vult, nolumus, non vultis, nolunt *(I am not willing, you are not willing, he is not willing, we are not willing, you are not willing, they are not willing)**

**Just memorize this word and its meanings for now.*

Remember your rules for gender:

> **Feminine nouns usually end in s-o-x**
>
> **Neuter nouns usually end in l-a-n-c-e-t**
>
> **Masculine nouns end in er-r-or**
> **Words that clearly denote a person of a particular gender are in that gender.**
> **(Ex: Cicero is masculine)**

Remember the Latin names for English cases and how to get them:

> **Nominative = Subject = First Form**
>
> **Genitive = Possessive = Second Form**
>
> **Accusative = Direct Object = Stem + em**

There are special words called prepositions. Here are some of these words:

into	to	across	through	towards	against
before	after	by	with	from	out of
in	on	of	for		

Prepositions relate a noun to another word, like a noun or verb. They are always followed by a noun — that is, by a word that is a person, place, or thing. Let's look at an example:

The fish swims **in** the water.

Explanation: "in" is the preposition. "Water" is the word that follows it (because "the" doesn't really count, does it?) We call "water" the object of the preposition.

John hit the ball **into** the water.

Explanation: "into" is the preposition. "Water" is the word that follows it (because "the" doesn't really count, does it?) We call "water" the object of the preposition.

Day 1, Exercise 1: Circle the prepositions in the following sentences. Underline the objects of the prepositions:

(prepositions are boxed)

1. The ball is [from] <u>Matt</u>.
2. The boy jumped [in] the <u>water</u>.
3. The boy jumped [into] the <u>water</u>.
4. Peter went [on] an <u>expedition</u>.
5. I ate dinner [with] <u>Sophia</u>.
6. I saw the gate [of] the <u>garden</u>.
7. You should start [before] <u>me</u>.
8. [By] <u>noon</u>, they will be here.

Day 1, Exercise 2: Do a complete synopsis of the verb "bibere". The following chart will help.

3rd Present	4th Present	3rd Past	4th Past
rego	audio	regebam	audiebam
regis	audis	regebas	audiebas
regit	audit	regebat	audiebat
regimus	audimus	regebamus	audiebamus
regitis	auditis	regebatis	audiebatis
regunt	audiunt	regebant	audiebant

3rd Future Regular	4th Future Regular	3rd Future Possibles	4th Future Possibles
regam	audiam	regam	audiam
reges	audies	regas	audias
reget	audiet	regat	audiat
regemus	audiemus	regamus	audiamus
regetis	audietis	regatis	audiatis
regent	audient	regant	audiant

(This exercise is continued on the next page.)

A verb that loves its i will keep it, but otherwise it copycats the -ere verbs. It doesn't have to change the "e" to "i" for the present, because it is already an "i". However, it adds the "e" for the past and future, so it can be just like the third conjugation -ere words, but it doesn't lose its "i". It loves its "i". The future possible changes the "e" of the regular to an "a".

	Present	Past	Future Regulars	Future Possibles
1st Singular	bibo	bibebam	bibam	bibam
2nd Singular	bibis	bibebas	bibes	bibas
3rd Singular	bibit	bibebat	bibet	bibat
1st Plural	bibimus	bibebamus	bibemus	bibamus
2nd Plural	bibitis	bibebatis	bibetis	bibatis
3rd Plural	bibunt	bibebant	bibent	bibant

Remember last week, we noticed that "of" and "for" were the two prepositions that you were not given the Latin words for. That is because there is no Latin word for these two prepositions. Do you ignore them in Latin? No! They are not like the words "the", "a", and "an" which we do ignore. "For" and "of" are indicator words. They tell us what case to put their objects in. Today we will learn about the case you put the object of the word "of" in. And that case is the genitive/possessive case. So, remember up until now, you knew to put a word in the genitive/possessive case because it had an **'s** on the end of it. Now you know that you also put a word in the genitive/possessive case because it follows the word "of".

The words in bold are genitive/possessive: **Mary's** dog   the dog of **Mary**

Day 2, Exercise 1: Box all the possessives. There is one in each sentence.

1. |Mary's| ball is green.
2. |Pike's| Peak is famous.
3. The |dog's| collar was missing.
4. The salad of the |day| is good.
5. The house of the |president| is big.
6. He was the man of the |hour|.
7. The meow of the |cat| sounded weird.
8. The |cricket's| song was pretty

Day 2, Exercise 2: Fill in the charts:

	Word	Meaning
1st Singular	possum	I am able
2nd Singular	potes	you are able
3rd Singular	potest	he is able
1st Plural	possumus	we are able
2nd Plural	potestis	you are able
3rd Plural	possunt	they are able

	Word	Meaning
1st Singular	eram	I was
2nd Singular	eras	you were
3rd Singular	erat	he was
1st Plural	eramus	we were
2nd Plural	eratis	you were
3rd Plural	erant	they were

Day 3, Exercise 1: Give the genitive form in Latin for each of the following words that should be genitive. (To do this, first box the word that is in the genitive/possessive case. You did this in Exercise 3.) Remember that the second form of each noun in your vocabulary is the genitive/possessive form.

Example: The tree's branch.   **arboris**

1. The dog's house   ***canis***

2. The city of Caesar   ***Caesaris***

3. The city's water   ***urbis***

4. Cicero's food   ***Ciceronis***

5. The light of the sun   ***solis***

6. The sun's light   ***solis***

7. The law of the city   ***urbis***

8. The tribe's river   ***gentis***

Day 3, Exercise 2: Translate, following these steps.

Step 1: Please circle the subject, box the possessives and underline the direct objects. Cross out the words, "the," "a," or "an."

Step 2: Write the Latin word you would use on line A above the word. Remember that there is no Latin word for "the," "a," or "an."

Step 3: Write the stem of the words (which need the stem form) on line B.

Step 4: Add the correct endings to complete the translation on line C.

(This exercise is continued on the next page.)

Now let's apply these steps to the first sentence below: *The man will believe Caesar*.

> Step 1: Please circle the subject, box the possessives and underline the direct objects. Cross out the words, "the," "a," or "an."

a) Locate the verb. It has a shaded box below it. So in this sentence it is "will believe".

b) Ask yourself "Who/what will believe?" Answer: Man. "Man" is the subject; circle it.

c) The man will believe whom/what? Answer: Caesar. "Caesar" is the direct object; underline it.

d) Are there any possessives? These words have 's in them. In this sentence, there are none.

e) Cross out any "the", "a", or "an"s. So, cross out the word "the" in this sentence.

> Step 2: Write the Latin word you would use on line A above the word. Remember that there is no Latin word for "the," "a," or "an."

On line "A", write the words as they appear in your vocabulary. Put "NA" for any words that are not translated. So, you would have:

The = NA (line A)

man = homo, hominis (line A)

will believe = credere (line A)

Caesar = Caesar, Caesaris (line A)

(Continued on the next page.)

> Step 3: Write the stem of the words (which need the stem form) on line B.

You only have to write the stem for words that need the stem to build the word. So, in this case put the stem down for credere (crede) and Caesar, Caesaris (Caesar).

> Step 4: Add the correct endings to complete the translation on line C.

The correct form of "homo, hominis" is the first form, which is the nominative form used for the subject. So it is **homo**.

The correct form of "Caesar, Caesaris" is the stem + em, which is the accusative form used for the direct object. So it is **Caesarem.**

The shaded box reminds you this is a verb word so think about these things when you translate that word.

a) What is the tense? **Answer: future.**

b) What do you do to the stem because of that tense? For example, change e to i to get the present for an -ere word.) Answer: Leave it alone.

c) What personal ending do you use? (In other words is "man" an "I," "you," "he," "she," or "it.") Plug in your word in the shaded box. Answer: "t" for "he". Word is "credet."

1.

A. *NA lex, legis*   *NA   civitas, civitatis*   *regere*   *NA gens, gentis*

B.   *rege*   *gent*

~~The~~ (law) of ~~the~~   [state]   rules   ~~the~~   tribe.

C.   *Lex*   *civitatis*   *regit*   *gentem.*

(This exercise is continued on the next page.)

2.

A.	***Caesar, Caesaris***	***munire***	***NA***	***urbs, urbis***
B.		***muni***		***urb***
	(Caesar)	will build*	~~the~~	city.
C.	***Caesar***	***muniet***		***urbem.***

* Remember i-lovers keep their "i" always. They also copycat the -ere verbs.

3.

A.	***Caesar, Caesaris***	***canis, canis***	***edere***	***NA***	***panis, panis***
B.			***ede***		***pan***
	Caesar's	(dog)	was eating	the	bread
C.	***Caesaris***	***canis***	***edebat***		***panem***

Lesson XI

Go over these every day for 10 minutes. New words are in bold.

VERBS

laudare	to praise	monēre	to warn
audire	to hear	agere	to act, to do
bibere	to drink	edere	to eat
vivere	to live	ponere	to put, to place
regere	to rule	vincere	to conquer
credere	to believe	ducere	to lead
currere	to run	mittere	to send
defendere	to defend	scribere	to write
sentire	to feel	munire	to build
dicere	to say	**petere**	**to seek**

NOUNS

dolor, doloris	pain, sorrow	panis, panis (m)	bread
mons, montis (m)	mountain	crux, crucis	cross
homo, hominis (m)	man	urbs, urbis	city
flumen, fluminis	river	civitas, civitatis	state
pax, pacis	peace	caput, capitis	head
Caesar, Caesaris	Caesar	Cicero, Ciceronis (m)	Cicero
canis, canis (m/f)	dog	veritas, veritatis	truth
virgo, virginis	virgin	arbor, arboris (f)	tree
sol, solis (m)	sun	rex, regis (m)	king
tempus, temporis (n)	time	civis, civis (m/f)	citizen
dux, ducis (m)	leader	lux, lucis	light
lex, legis	law	gens, gentis	tribe
fons, fontis (m)	fountain	tentatio, tentationis	temptation
caritas, caritatis	love	libertas, libertatis	freedom, liberty
pastor, pastoris	shepherd	**mare, maris**	**sea**

SPECIAL INDECLINABLE* WORDS:

non	not	diu	for a long time
saepe	often	in	into, onto
in	in, on	trans	across
ad	to, towards	contra	against
per	through	post	after
ante	before	cum	with
a, ab	by	e, ex	out of
de	from		

* Indeclinable means they never change. They never change even an ending.

-o, or -m	I	-mus	we
-s	you (sing)	-tis	you
-t	he, she, or it	-nt	they

sum, es, est, sumus, estis, sunt *(I am, you are, he is, we are, you are, they are)*

eram, eras, erat, eramus, eratis, erant *(I was, you were, he was, we were, you were, they were)*

ero, eris, erit, erimus, eritis, erunt *(I will be, you will be, he will be, we will be, you will be, they will be)*

possum, potes, potest, possumus, potestis, possunt *(I am able, you are able, he is able, we are able, you are able, they are able)*

poteram, poteras, poterat, poteramus, poteratis, poterant *(I was able, you were able, he was able, we were able, you were able, they were able)*

potero, poteris, poterit, poterimus, poteritis, poterunt *(I will be able, you will be able, he will be able, we will be able, you will be able, they will be able)*

volo, vis, vult, volumus, vultis, volunt *(I am willing, you are willing, he is willing, we are willing, you are willing, they are willing)*

nolo, non vis, non vult, nolumus, non vultis, nolunt *(I am not willing, you are not willing, he is not willing, we are not willing, you are not willing, they are not willing)*

Remember your rules for gender:

> **Feminine nouns usually end in s-o-x**
>
> **Neuter nouns usually end in l-a-n-c-e-t**
>
> **Masculine nouns end in er-r-or**
>
> **Words that clearly denote a person of a particular gender are in that gender.**
>
> **(Ex: Cicero is masculine)**

Remember the Latin names for English cases and how to get them:

> **Nominative = Subject = First Form**
>
> **Genitive = Possessive ('s or the object of "of") = Second Form**
>
> **Accusative = Direct Object = Stem + em**

You noted that two of the preposition words were special, "of" and "for". Last week you learned that the object of the preposition "of" is in the genitive. You know that "of" is not translated.

Well today you will learn that the object of the preposition "for" takes the dative/indirect object case. This is a new case. The indirect object is "for whom" an action is done. Sometimes "for" is used to express for what (purpose or end, or for whose advantage/disadvantage something is done.)

Example: Mary baked a cake for mom

Mary baked a cake for whom? mom. Mom is the indirect object.

Example: Caesar used a sword for battle.

For what purpose did Caesar use a sword? battle. Battle is in the case of the dative/indirect object.

Beginning Latin II - Lesson XI

Day 1, Exercise 1: Every sentence below has the preposition "for" or "of" in it. Please underline the objects of the prepositions and say if they are dative or genitive. Remember genitive objects of prepositions follow "of" and dative objects of prepositions follow "for".

1. John bought flowers for **mom**.   **_dative_**   genitive

2. John has a job for **me**.   **_dative_**   genitive

3. Mary saw the house of **Lincoln**.   dative   **_genitive_**

4. The color of the **flowers** was red.   dative   **_genitive_**

5. The cake is for the **children**.   **_dative_**   genitive

Day 1, Exercise 2: Do a complete synopsis of the verb "petere". The following chart will help.

3rd Present	4th Present	3rd Past	4th Past
rego	audio	regebam	audiebam
regis	audis	regebas	audiebas
regit	audit	regebat	audiebat
regimus	audimus	regebamus	audiebamus
regitis	auditis	regebatis	audiebatis
regunt	audiunt	regebant	audiebant

3rd Future Regular	4th Future Regular	3rd Future Possibles	4th Future Possibles
regam	audiam	regam	audiam
reges	audies	regas	audias
reget	audiet	regat	audiat
regemus	audiemus	regamus	audiamus
regetis	audietis	regatis	audiatis
regent	audient	regant	audiant

Beginning Latin II - Lesson XI

> -ere verbs change the "e" to an "i" for the present, and then add the endings. They add "ba" and the endings to the stem to make the past. They just add the endings to the stem to make the future.
>
> A verb that loves its i will keep it, but otherwise it copycats the -ere verbs. It doesn't have to change the "e" to "i" for the present, because it is already an "i". However, it adds the "e" for the past and future, so it can be just like the -ere words, but it doesn't lose it "i". It loves its "i"s.

	Present	Past	Future Regulars	Future Possibles
1st Singular	peto	petebam	petam	petam
2nd Singular	petis	petebas	petes	petas
3rd Singular	petit	petebat	petet	petat
1st Plural	petimus	petebamus	petemus	petamus
2nd Plural	petitis	petebatis	petetis	petatis
3rd Plural	petunt	petebant	petent	petant

Forming the dative case in Latin is pretty easy. Here is the rule.

| Dative = Indirect Object = Stem + i |

Day 2, Exercise 1: Give the dative of the following nouns.

A. civitas, civitatis — *civitati*

B. pax, pacis — *paci*

C. flumen, fluminis — *flumini*

D. mare, maris — *mari*

E. canis, canis — *cani*

F. arbor, arboris — *arbori*

Day 2, Exercise 2: Fill in the charts:

	Word	Meaning
1st Singular	sum	I am
2nd Singular	es	you are
3rd Singular	est	he is
1st Plural	sumus	we are
2nd Plural	estis	you are
3rd Plural	sunt	they are

(This exercise is continued on the next page.)

	Word	Meaning
1st Singular	ero	*I will be*
2nd Singular	eris	*you will be*
3rd Singular	erit	*he will be*
1st Plural	erimus	*we will be*
2nd Plural	eritis	*you will be*
3rd Plural	erunt	*they will be*

Day 3, Exercise 1: Translate the following underlined words. To do so, remember that "of" takes the genitive possessive and "for" takes the dative.

Example: bread <u>for Caesar</u>   <u>**Caesari**</u>

1. house <u>for the dog</u>   <u>***cani***</u>

2. house <u>of the dog</u>   <u>***canis***</u>

3. water <u>of the river</u>   <u>***fluminis***</u>

4. food <u>for Cicero</u>   <u>***Ciceroni***</u>

5. food <u>of the man</u>   <u>***hominis***</u>

6. The light <u>of the cross</u>   <u>***crucis***</u>

7. The law <u>for the state</u>   <u>***civitati***</u>

8. town <u>for Caesar</u>   <u>***Caesari***</u>

Day 3, Exercise 2: Translate following these steps:

> Step 1: Please circle the subject, box the possessives and underline the <u>direct objects</u>. Use a dashed line under the indirect object. Cross out the words, "the," "a," or "an."
>
> Step 2: Write the Latin word you would use on Line A above the word. Remember that there is no Latin word for "of," "for," "the," "a," or "an."
>
> Step 3: Write the stem of the words (which need the stem form) on line B.
>
> Step 4: Add the correct endings to complete the translation on line C.

Now let's apply these steps to the first sentence below: <u>*The man will believe Caesar's law for Cicero.*</u>

> Step 1: Please circle the subject, box the possessives and underline the direct objects. Cross out the words, "the," "a," or "an."

a) Locate the verb. It has a shaded box below it. So in this sentence it is "will believe

b) Ask yourself "Who/what will believe?" Answer: Man. "Man" is the subject; circle it.

c) The man will believe whom/what? Answer: Law. "Law" is the direct object; underline it.

d) Are there any possessives? These words have 's in them or they are the object of "of." Answer: Yes, Caesar is the possessive. Box Caesar's.

e) Ask yourself "The man will believe law for whom/what purpose?" Answer: Cicero. "Cicero" is the indirect object. Dash underline under the word Cicero.

f) Now, cross out any "the," "a," or "an"s. So, cross out the word "the" in this sentence.

(This exercise is continued on the next page.)

> **Step 2:** Write the Latin word you would use on Line A above the word. Remember that there is no Latin word for "the," "a," or "an."

On line "A", write the words as they appear in your vocabulary. Put "NA" for any words that are not translated. So, you would have:

The = NA (line A)

man = homo, hominis (line A)

will believe = credere (line A)

Caesar's = Caesar, Caesaris (line A)

law = lex, legis (line A)

for = NA (line A)

Cicero = Cicero, Ciceronis (line A)

> **Step 3:** Write the stem of the words (which need the stem form) on line B.

You only have to write the stem for words that need the stem to build the word. So, in this case put the stem down for credere (crede) and lex, legis (leg-) and Cicero, Ciceronis (Ciceron-).

> **Step 4:** Add the correct endings to complete the translation on line C.

The correct form of "homo, hominis" is the first form, which is the nominative form used for the subject. So it is **homo**.

The correct form of "Caesar, Caesaris" is the second form, which is the genitive form used for the possessive. So it is **Caesaris.**

(This exercise is continued on the next page.)

The correct form of "lex, legis" is the stem + em, which is the accusative form used for the direct object. So it is **legem.**

The correct form of "Cicero, Ciceronis" is the stem + i, which is the dative form used for the indirect object. So it is **Ciceroni.**

The shaded box reminds you this is a verb word so think about these things when you translate that word.

a) What is the tense? *Answer: future.*

b) What do you do to the stem because of that tense? For example, change e to i to get the present for an -ere word.) *Answer: Leave it alone.*

c) What personal ending do you use? (In other words is "man" an "I," "you," "he," "she," or "it.") Plug in your word in the shaded box. *Answer: "t" for "he". Word is "credet."*

1.

A.	*NA*	*gens, gentis*	*petere*	*Caesar, Caesaris*	*NA*	*pax, pacis*
B.			*pete*	*Caesar*		*pac*
	~~The~~	(tribe)	seeks	Caesar	for	peace
C.		*Gens*	*petit*	*Caesarem*		*paci*

(This exercise is continued on the next page.)

2.

A. **_Cicero, Ciceronis_**   **_audire_**   **_NA_**   **_fons, fontis_**

B.   **_audi_**   **_font_**

   (Cicero)   will hear*   ~~the~~   fountain.

C. **_Cicero_**   **_audiet_**   **_fontem_**

* Remember i-lovers keep their "i" always. They also copycat the -ere verbs.

3.

A.   **_NA_**   **_pastor, pastoris_**   **_canis, canis_**   **_bibere_**

B.   **_bibe_**

   ~~The~~   shepherd's   (dog)   was drinking.

C.   **_pastoris_**   **_canis_**   **_bibebat_**

Lesson XII

Go over these every day for 10 minutes.

VERBS

laudare	to praise	monēre	to warn
audire	to hear	agere	to act, to do
bibere	to drink	edere	to eat
vivere	to live	ponere	to put, to place
regere	to rule	vincere	to conquer
credere	to believe	ducere	to lead
currere	to run	mittere	to send
defendere	to defend	scribere	to write
sentire	to feel	munire	to build
dicere	to say	petere	to seek

NOUNS

dolor, doloris	pain, sorrow	panis, panis (m)	bread
mons, montis (m)	mountain	crux, crucis	cross
homo, hominis (m)	man	urbs, urbis	city
flumen, fluminis	river	civitas, civitatis	state
pax, pacis	peace	caput, capitis	head
Caesar, Caesaris	Caesar	Cicero, Ciceronis (m)	Cicero
canis, canis (m/f)	dog	veritas, veritatis	truth
virgo, virginis	virgin	arbor, arboris (f)	tree
sol, solis (m)	sun	rex, regis (m)	king
tempus, temporis (n)	time	civis, civis (m/f)	citizen
dux, ducis (m)	leader	lux, lucis	light
lex, legis	law	gens, gentis	tribe
fons, fontis (m)	fountain	tentatio, tentationis	temptation
caritas, caritatis	love	libertas, libertatis	freedom, liberty
pastor, pastoris	shepherd	mare, maris	sea

SPECIAL INDECLINABLE* WORDS:

non	not	diu	for a long time
saepe	often	in	into, onto
in	in, on	trans	across
ad	to, towards	contra	against
per	through	post	after
ante	before	cum	with
a, ab	by	e, ex	out of
de	from		

* Indeclinable means they never change. They never change even an ending.

-o, or -m	I	-mus	we
-s	you (sing)	-tis	you
-t	he, she, or it	-nt	they

sum, es, est, sumus, estis, sunt *(I am, you are, he is, we are, you are, they are)*

eram, eras, erat, eramus, eratis, erant *(I was, you were, he was, we were, you were, they were)*

ero, eris, erit, erimus, eritis, erunt *(I will be, you will be, he will be, we will be, you will be, they will be)*

possum, potes, potest, possumus, potestis, possunt *(I am able, you are able, he is able, we are able, you are able, they are able)*

poteram, poteras, poterat, poteramus, poteratis, poterant *(I was able, you were able, he was able, we were able, you were able, they were able)*

potero, poteris, poterit, poterimus, poteritis, poterunt *(I will be able, you will be able, he will be able, we will be able, you will be able, they will be able)*

volo, vis, vult, volumus, vultis, volunt *(I am willing, you are willing, he is willing, we are willing, you are willing, they are willing)*

nolo, non vis, non vult, nolumus, non vultis, nolunt *(I am not willing, you are not willing, he is not willing, we are not willing, you are not willing, they are not willing)*

Remember your rules for gender:

> **Feminine nouns usually end in s-o-x**
>
> **Neuter nouns usually end in l-a-n-c-e-t**
>
> **Masculine nouns end in -er-r-or**
>
> **Words that clearly denote a person of a particular gender are in that gender.**
>
> **(Ex: Cicero is masculine)**

Remember the Latin names for English cases and how to get them:

> **Nominative = Subject = First Form**
>
> **Genitive = Possessive ('s or the object of "of") = Second Form**
>
> **Dative = Indirect Object = Stem + i**
>
> **Accusative = Direct Object = Stem + em**

You learned that two of the preposition words were special, "of" and "for". Last week you learned that the object of the preposition "for" is in the dative. You know that "for" is not translated. You learned that "for" indicated the dative/indirect object, which is the word that answers "for what (purpose, advantage/disadvantage)" or "for whom".

Did you know that sometimes you don't need the word "for" to ask the question "for whom?" To show this let me use our examples from last week.

Example: Mary baked a cake for mom.

Mary baked a cake for whom? Mom.   Mom is the indirect object.

Now, watch this:

Mary baked mom a cake. *(See, I put mom before cake.)*

Mary baked what? Did she bake mom or the cake? The answer is the cake. So, the cake is still the direct object. *Mary baked a cake for whom?* The answer is still mom.

(This exercise is continued on the next page.)

Now let's look at another example.

Example: Caesar used a sword for battle.

For what (purpose or advantage did Caesar use a sword? battle. Battle is in the same case as the indirect object.

Now, watch this:

Caesar used the battle a sword.

Yikes! Who would say that? But if someone did, it is still true that sword is the direct object. Caesar used what? Did he use the sword or the battle? The answer is the sword. So, the sword is still the direct object. Caesar used a sword for what reason or purpose? The answer is still battle.

Day 1, Exercise 1: The subjects are circled and the possessives are boxed. Now you underline the direct objects and dash underline the indirect objects. Remember the direct objects answer "whom" or "what" about the verb! The indirect object is the "for whom" or "for what (purpose)" something was done.

1. John's (cat) chased the dog for fun.

John's cat chased what? ***dog***   for what purpose? ***fun***

2. (John) chased the cat for the dog.

John chased what? ***cat***   for whom? ***dog***

3. The (girls) ran to the river. (NA might be an answer.)

The (girls) ran what? ***(NA)*** for whom? ***(NA)***

4. The (cook) cooked his friend a mince pie for dessert.

The cook cooked what? ***mince pie***   for whom? ***friend***

for what (purpose)? ***dessert***

Day 1, Exercise 2: Let's write all the cases of Latin nouns that we know in order.

Example: lex, legis

Nominative = Subject = First Form = **_lex_**

Genitive = Possessive = Second Form = **_legis_**

Dative = Indirect Object = Stem + i = **_legi_**

Accusative = Direct Object = Stem + em = **_legem_**

A. lux, lucis

Nominative = Subject = First Form = **_lux_**

Genitive = Possessive = Second Form = **_lucis_**

Dative = Indirect Object = Stem + i = **_luci_**

Accusative = Direct Object = Stem + em = **_lucem_**

B. caritas, caritatis

Nominative = Subject = First Form = **_caritas_**

Genitive = Possessive = Second Form = **_caritatis_**

Dative = Indirect Object = Stem + i = **_caritati_**

Accusative = Direct Object = Stem + em = **_caritatem_**

C. mons, montis

Nominative = Subject = First Form = **_mons_**

Genitive = Possessive = Second Form = **_montis_**

Dative = Indirect Object = Stem + i = **_monti_**

Accusative = Direct Object = Stem + em = **_montem_**

D. crux, crucis

Nominative = Subject = First Form = **_crux_**

Genitive = Possessive = Second Form = **_crucis_**

Dative = Indirect Object = Stem + i = **_cruci_**

Accusative = Direct Object = Stem + em = **_crucem_**

Day 2, Exercise 1: Do a complete synopsis of the verb "ducere". The following chart will help.

3rd Present	4th Present	3rd Past	4th Past
rego	audio	regebam	audiebam
regis	audis	regebas	audiebas
regit	audit	regebat	audiebat
regimus	audimus	regebamus	audiebamus
regitis	auditis	regebatis	audiebatis
regunt	audiunt	regebant	audiebant

3rd Future Regular	4th Future Regular	3rd Future Possibles	4th Future Possibles
regam	audiam	regam	audiam
reges	audies	regas	audias
reget	audiet	regat	audiat
regemus	audiemus	regamus	audiamus
regetis	audietis	regatis	audiatis
regent	audient	regant	audiant

> **A verb that loves its i will keep it, but otherwise it copycats the -ere verbs. It doesn't have to change the "e" to "i" for the present, because it is already an "i." However, it adds the "e" for the past and future, so it can be just like the third conjugation -ere words, but it doesn't lose its "i." It loves its "i." The future possible changes the "e" of the regular to an "a."**

(This exercise is continued on the next page.)

	Present	Past	Future	
			Regulars	Possibles
1st Singular	duco	ducebam	ducam	ducam
2nd Singular	ducis	ducebas	duces	ducas
3rd Singular	ducit	ducebat	ducet	ducat
1st Plural	ducimus	ducebamus	ducemus	ducamus
2nd Plural	ducitis	ducebatis	ducetis	ducatis
3rd Plural	ducunt	ducebant	ducent	ducant

Day 2, Exercise 2: Match from memory.
(Match column 1 to column 2 and column 2 to column 3).

nominative *(first form)*	stem + em *(direct object)*	possessive
genitive *(second form)*	first form *(subject)*	indirect object
dative *(stem + i)*	stem + i *(indirect object)*	subject
accusative *(stem + em)*	second form *(possessive)*	direct object

Day 3, Exercise 1: Fill in the charts.

	Word	Meaning
1st Singular	*volo*	I am willing
2nd Singular	*vis*	you are willing
3rd Singular	*vult*	he is willing
1st Plural	*volumus*	we are willing
2nd Plural	*vultis*	you are willing
3rd Plural	*volunt*	they are willing

	Word	Meaning
1st Singular	potero	*I will be able*
2nd Singular	poteris	*you will be able*
3rd Singular	poterit	*he will be able*
1st Plural	poterimus	*we will be able*
2nd Plural	poteritis	*you will be able*
3rd Plural	poterunt	*they will be able*

Day 3, Exercise 2: Translate following these steps:

> Step 1: Please circle the subject, box the possessives and underline the <u>direct objects</u>. Use a dashed line under the indirect object. Cross out the words, "the," "a," or "an."
>
> Step 2: Write the Latin word you would use on Line A above the word. Remember that there is no Latin word for "of," "for," "the," "a," or "an."
>
> Step 3: Write the stem of the words (which need the stem form) on line B.
>
> Step 4: Add the correct endings to complete the translation on line C.

Now let's apply these steps to the first sentence below: <u>*The man will believe Caesar's law for Cicero.*</u>

> Step 1: Please circle the subject, box the possessives and underline the direct objects. Cross out the words, "the," "a," or "an."

a) Locate the verb. It has a shaded box below it. So in this sentence it is "will believe".

b) Ask yourself "Who/what will believe?" Answer: Man. "Man" is the subject; circle it.

c) The man will believe whom/what? Answer: Law. "Law" is the direct object; underline it.

d) Are there any possessives? These words have 's in them or they are the object of "of." Answer: Yes, "Caesar" is the possessive. Box "Caesar's".

e) Ask yourself "The man will believe law for whom/what purpose?" Answer: Cicero. "Cicero" is the indirect object. Dash underline under the word "Cicero".

f) Now, cross out any "the," "a," or "an"s. So, cross out the word "the" in this sentence.

(This exercise is continued on the next page.)

> Step 2: Write the Latin word you would use on Line A above the word. Remember that there is no Latin word for "the," "a," or "an."

On line "A", write the words as they appear in your vocabulary. Put "NA" for any words that are not translated. So, you would have:

The = NA (line A)

man = homo, hominis (line A)

will believe = credere (line A)

Caesar's = Caesar, Caesaris (line A)

law = lex, legis (line A)

for = NA (line A)

Cicero = Cicero, Ciceronis (line A)

> Step 3: Write the stem of the words (which need the stem form) on line B.

You only have to write the stem for words that need the stem to build the word. So, in this case put the stem down for credere (crede-) and lex, legis (leg-) and Cicero, Ciceronis (Ciceron-).

> Step 4: Add the correct endings to complete the translation on line C.

The correct form of "homo, hominis" is the first form, which is the nominative form used for the subject. So it is **homo**.

The correct form of "Caesar, Caesaris" is the second form, which is the genitive form used for the possessive. So it is **Caesaris.**

(This exercise is continued on the next page.)

The correct form of "lex, legis" is the stem + em, which is the accusative form used for the direct object. So it is **legem.**

The correct form of "Cicero, Ciceronis" is the stem + i, which is the dative form used for the indirect object. So it is **Ciceroni.**

The shaded box reminds you this is a verb word so think about these things when you translate that word.

a) What is the tense? *Answer: future.*

b) What do you do to the stem because of that tense? for example, change e to i to get the present for an -ere word.) *Answer: Leave it alone.*

c) What personal ending do you use? (In other words is "man" an "I," "you," "he," "she," or "it.") Plug in your word in the shaded box. *Answer: "t" for "he". Word is "credet."*

1.

	A. <u>*NA*</u>	<u>*pastor, pastoris*</u>	<u>*petere*</u>	<u>*libertas, libertatis*</u>	<u>*NA*</u>	<u>*homo, hominis*</u>
	B.		<u>*pete*</u>	<u>*libertat*</u>		<u>*homin*</u>
	~~The~~	shepherd	may seek	<u>freedom</u>	for	<u>man</u>
	C.	<u>*Pastor*</u>	<u>*petat*</u>	<u>*libertatem*</u>		<u>*homini*</u>

2.

	A. <u>*Cicero, Ciceronis*</u>	<u>*defendere*</u>	<u>*NA*</u>	<u>*veritas, veritatis*</u>
	B.	<u>*defende*</u>		<u>*veritat*</u>
	(Cicero)	will defend	~~the~~	<u>truth</u>
	C. <u>*Cicero*</u>	<u>*defendet*</u>		<u>*veritatem*</u>

Lesson XIII

Go over these every day for 10 minutes. New words are in bold.

VERBS

laudare	to praise	monēre	to warn
audire	to hear	agere	to act, to do
bibere	to drink	edere	to eat
vivere	to live	ponere	to put, to place
regere	to rule	vincere	to conquer
credere	to believe	ducere	to lead
currere	to run	mittere	to send
defendere	to defend	scribere	to write
sentire	to feel	munire	to build
dicere	to say	petere	to seek

NOUNS

dolor, doloris	pain, sorrow	panis, panis (m)	bread
mons, montis (m)	mountain	crux, crucis	cross
homo, hominis (m)	man	urbs, urbis	city
flumen, fluminis	river	civitas, civitatis	state
pax, pacis	peace	caput, capitis	head
Caesar, Caesaris	Caesar	Cicero, Ciceronis (m)	Cicero
canis, canis (m/f)	dog	veritas, veritatis	truth
virgo, virginis	virgin	arbor, arboris (f)	tree
sol, solis (m)	sun	rex, regis (m)	king
tempus, temporis (n)	time	civis, civis (m/f)	citizen
dux, ducis (m)	leader	lux, lucis	light
lex, legis	law	gens, gentis	tribe
fons, fontis (m)	fountain	tentatio, tentationis	temptation
caritas, caritatis	love	libertas, libertatis	freedom, liberty
pastor, pastoris	shepherd	mare, maris	sea

Beginning Latin II - Lesson XIII

SPECIAL INDECLINABLE* WORDS:

non	not	diu	for a long time
saepe	often	**bene**	**well**
in (ablative)	in, on	in (accusative)	into, onto
ad (accusative)	to, towards	trans (accusative)	across
per (accusative)	through	contra (accusative)	against
ante (accusative)	before	post (accusative)	after
a, ab (ablative)	by	cum (ablative)	with
de (ablative)	from, down from	e, ex (ablative)	out of

Indeclinable means they never change. They never change even an ending.

-o, or -m	I	-mus	we
-s	you (sing)	-tis	you
-t	he, she, or it	-nt	they

sum, es, est, sumus, estis, sunt *(I am, you are, he is, we are, you are, they are)*

eram, eras, erat, eramus, eratis, erant *(I was, you were, he was, we were, you were, they were)*

ero, eris, erit, erimus, eritis, erunt *(I will be, you will be, he will be, we will be, you will be, they will be)*

possum, potes, potest, possumus, potestis, possunt *(I am able, you are able, he is able, we are able, you are able, they are able)*

poteram, poteras, poterat, poteramus, poteratis, poterant *(I was able, you were able, he was able, we were able, you were able, they were able)*

potero, poteris, poterit, poterimus, poteritis, poterunt *(I will be able, you will be able, he will be able, we will be able, you will be able, they will be able)*

volo, vis, vult, volumus, vultis, volunt *(I am willing, you are willing, he is willing, we are willing, you are willing, they are willing)*

nolo, non vis, non vult, nolumus, non vultis, nolunt *(I am not willing, you are not willing, he is not willing, we are not willing, you are not willing, they are not willing)*

Remember your rules for gender:

> **Feminine nouns usually end in s-o-x**
>
> **Neuter nouns usually end in l-a-n-c-e-t**
>
> **Masculine nouns end in er-r-or**
> **Words that clearly denote a person of a particular gender are in that gender.**
> **(Ex: Cicero is masculine)**

Did you notice on your list of vocabulary that your prepositions all have the word "accusative" or "ablative" after them? That tells you whether that preposition will be followed by a word in the accusative or ablative case. The ablative is a new case. You will use it for objects of some prepositions. The object is the word that follows the preposition. The accusative is used for some objects of prepositions as well. So if you have a sentence like "the fish is in the water" you would say that "in" is the preposition and "water" is its object (that is the word following it.) (Remember we don't count "the" as a word in Latin.)

So review your new chart. Notice the additions to the accusative case and the notice the ablative case is on this chart now too. So now you have two ways you can use accusatives!

> **Nominative = Subject = First Form**
>
> **Genitive = Possessive ('s or the object of "of") = Second Form**
>
> **Dative = Indirect Object (object of "for") = Stem + i**
>
> **Accusative = Direct Object or Object of some prepositions = Stem + em**
>
> **Ablative = Object of some prepositions = Stem + e**

Day 1, Exercise 1: Use the vocabulary list to determine which of the objects of the prepositions (in parentheses) are ablative and which are accusative. To do this well, put an "x" above the preposition word first. Then find that word on the vocabulary list and see what case the object of the preposition takes.

1. He walked <u>against</u> the (river).   ***accusative***   ablative
2. The dog ran <u>into</u> the (light).   ***accusative***   ablative
3. <u>By</u> (love), Christ conquered.   accusative   ***ablative***
4. Moses came <u>down from</u> the (mountain).   accusative   ***ablative***
5. The dog ran <u>after</u> the (shepherd).   ***accusative***   ablative

If you were to put these sentences into Latin, the case you circled would be the case you would put the words in parentheses.

Day 1, Exercise 2: Fill in the charts:

Latin Prepositions that take the Accusative Case	Latin Prepositions that take the Ablative Case
ad	*in*
per	*a, ab*
ante	*de*
in	*cum*
trans	*e, ex*
contra	
post	

What word is in both columns? ***in***

Which column has more words? ***Accusative column***

Day 2, Exercise 1: The subjects are circled and the possessives are boxed. Now you underline the accusative/direct objects and dash underline the dative/indirect objects. Remember the accusative answers "whom" or "what" about the verb. The dative is the "for whom" or "for what purpose" something was done.

1. (Sophie) sang a <u>song</u> for the p-e-o-p-l-e.

Sophie sang what? ***song***   for whom? ***people***

2. The [man's] (car) cost <s>the</s> m-o-t-h-e-r <u>money</u>.

The car cost what? ***money***   for whom? ***mother***

3. The (women) were saying a <u>prayer</u> for C-h-r-i-s-t.

The women were saying what? ***prayer***   for whom? ***Christ***

4. (He) begged for p-e-a-c-e. (Hint: Put NA on one line. Which one?)

He begged what? ***(NA)***   for what purpose? ***peace***

Rule for Ablative endings:

> **Ablative = Objects of some prepositions = Stem + e**

Day 2, Exercise 2: Let's write all the cases of Latin nouns that we know in order.

Example: lex, legis

Nominative = Subject = First Form =   <u>lex</u>

Genitive = Possessive = Second Form =   <u>legis</u>

Dative = Indirect Object = Stem + i =   <u>legi</u>

Accusative = Direct Object/Obj of Prepositions = Stem + em =   <u>legem</u>

Ablative = Obj of Prepositions = Stem + e =   <u>lege</u>

(This exercise is continued on the next page.)

A. veritas, veritatis

Nominative = Subject = First Form = **_veritas_**

Genitive = Possessive = Second Form = **_veritatis_**

Dative = Indirect Object = Stem + i = **_veritati_**

Accusative = Direct Object/Obj of Prepositions = Stem + em = **_veritatem_**

Ablative = Obj of Prepositions = Stem + e = **_veritate_**

B. civis, civis

Nominative = Subject = First Form = **_civis_**

Genitive = Possessive = Second Form = **_civis_**

Dative = Indirect Object = Stem + i = **_civi_**

Accusative = Direct Object/Obj of Prepositions = Stem + em = **_civem_**

Ablative = Obj of Prepositions = Stem + e = **_cive_**

C. lux, lucis

Nominative = Subject = First Form = **_lux_**

Genitive = Possessive = Second Form = **_lucis_**

Dative = Indirect Object = Stem + i = **_luci_**

Accusative = Direct Object/Obj of Prepositions = Stem + em = **_lucem_**

Ablative = Obj of Prepositions = Stem + e = **_luce_**

(This exercise is continued on the next page.)

D. crux, crucis

Nominative = Subject = First Form = **_crux_**

Genitive = Possessive = Second Form = **_crucis_**

Dative = Indirect Object = Stem + i = **_cruci_**

Accusative = Direct Object/Obj of Prepositions = Stem + em = **_crucem_**

Ablative = Obj of Prepositions = Stem + e = **_cruce_**

Day 3, Exercise 1: Do a complete synopsis of the verb "munire". The following chart will help.

3rd Present	4th Present	3rd Past	4th Past
rego	audio	regebam	audiebam
regis	audis	regebas	audiebas
regit	audit	regebat	audiebat
regimus	audimus	regebamus	audiebamus
regitis	auditis	regebatis	audiebatis
regunt	audiunt	regebant	audiebant
3rd Future Regular	4th Future Regular	3rd Future Possibles	4th Future Possibles
regam	audiam	regam	audiam
reges	audies	regas	audias
reget	audiet	regat	audiat
regemus	audiemus	regamus	audiamus
regetis	audietis	regatis	audiatis
regent	audient	regant	audiant

A verb that loves its i will keep it, but otherwise it copycats the -ere verbs. It doesn't have to change the "e" to "i" for the present, because it is already an "i". However, it adds the "e" for the past and future, so it can be just like the third conjugation -ere words, but it doesn't lose its "i". It loves its "i". The future possible changes the "e" of the regular to an "a".

	Present	Past	Future Regulars	Future Possibles
1st Singular	munio	muniebam	muniam	muniam
2nd Singular	munis	muniebas	munies	munias
3rd Singular	munit	muniebat	muniet	muniat
1st Plural	munimus	muniebamus	muniemus	muniamus
2nd Plural	munitis	muniebatis	munietis	muniatis
3rd Plural	muniunt	muniebant	munient	muniant

Day 3, Exercise 2: Translate following these steps:

Step 1: Please circle the subject, box the possessives and underline the direct objects. Use a dashed line under the indirect object. Cross out the words, "the," "a," or "an."

Step 2: Write the Latin word you would use on Line A above the word. Remember that there is no Latin word for "of," "for," "the," "a," or "an."

Step 3: Write the stem of the words (which need the stem form) on line B.

Step 4: Add the correct endings to complete the translation on line C.

(This exercise is continued on the next page.)

Now let's apply these steps to the first sentence below: *The man will believe Caesar's law for Cicero.*

> Step 1: Please circle the subject, box the possessives and underline the direct objects. Cross out the words, "the," "a," or "an."

a) Locate the verb. It has a shaded box below it. So in this sentence it is "will believe".

b) Ask yourself "Who/what will believe?" Answer: Man. "Man" is the subject; circle it.

c) The man will believe whom/what? Answer: Law. "Law" is the direct object; underline it.

d) Are there any possessives? These words have 's in them or they are the object of "of." Answer: Yes, Caesar is the possessive. Box Caesar's.

e) Ask yourself "The man will believe law for whom/what purpose?" Answer: Cicero. "Cicero" is the indirect object. Dash underline under the word Cicero.

f) Now, cross out any "the," "a," or "an"s. So, cross out the word "the" in this sentence.

> Step 2: Write the Latin word you would use on Line A above the word. Remember that there is no Latin word for "the," "a," or "an."

On line "A", write the words as they appear in your vocabulary. Put "NA" for any words that are not translated. So, you would have:

The = NA (line A)

man = homo, hominis (line A)

will believe = credere (line A)

Caesar's = Caesar, Caesaris (line A)

(This exercise is continued on the next page.)

law = lex, legis (line A)

for = NA (line A)

Cicero = Cicero, Ciceronis (line A)

> **Step 3: Write the stem of the words (which need the stem form) on line B.**

You only have to write the stem for words that need the stem to build the word. So, in this case put the stem down for credere (crede) and lex, legis (leg-) and Cicero, Ciceronis (Ciceron-).

> **Step 4: Add the correct endings to complete the translation on line C.**

The correct form of "homo, hominis" is the first form, which is the nominative form used for the subject. So it is **homo**.

The correct form of "Caesar, Caesaris" is the second form, which is the genitive form used for the possessive. So it is **Caesaris.**

The correct form of "lex, legis" is the stem + em, which is the accusative form used for the direct object. So it is **legem.**

The correct form of "Cicero, Ciceronis" is the stem + i, which is the dative form used for the indirect object. So it is **Ciceroni.**

The shaded box reminds you this is a verb word so think about these things when you translate that word.

a) What is the tense? **Answer: future.**

b) What do you do to the stem because of that tense? for example, change e to i to get the present for an -ere word.) Answer: Leave it alone.

c) What personal ending do you use? (In other words is "man" an "I," "you," "he," "she," or "it.") Plug in your word in the shaded box. Answer: "t" for "he". Word is "credet."

(This exercise is continued on the next page.)

1.

A. <u>**NA**</u> <u>**canis, canis**</u> <u>**edere**</u>   <u>**NA** **panis, panis**</u> <u>**NA**</u> <u>**NA** **virgo, virginis**</u>

B.   <u>**ede**</u>   <u>**pan**</u>   <u>**virgin**</u>

~~The~~   (dog)   may eat   ~~the~~   <u>bread</u>   for   ~~the~~   <u>v</u>ir<u>gin</u>.

C.   <u>**Canis**</u>   <u>**edat**</u>   <u>**panem**</u>   <u>**virgini.**</u>

2. Note: Observe how the preposition "across" and its object were done.

A. <u>***Cicero, Ciceronis***</u> <u>***mittere*** **NA** **panis, panis** **trans**</u>   <u>**NA** **mons, montis**</u>

B.   <u>**mitte**</u>   <u>**pan**</u>   (Accusative)   <u>mont-</u>

(Cicero)   was sending   ~~the~~   <u>bread</u>   across   ~~the~~   <u>mountain</u>

C. <u>***Cicero***</u>   <u>***mittebat***</u>   <u>***panem***</u>   trans   <u>montem.</u>

3. Note: Observe how the preposition "by" and its object were done.

A. <u>***Cicero, Ciceronis***</u> <u>***mittere***</u> <u>**NA**</u>   <u>**panis, panis**</u> ab <u>**NA** **mons, montis**</u>

B.   <u>**mitte**</u>   <u>**pan**</u>   (Ablative)   <u>mont</u>

(Cicero)   was sending   ~~the~~   <u>bread</u>   by   ~~the~~   <u>mountain</u>

C. <u>***Cicero***</u>   <u>***mittebat***</u>   <u>***panem***</u>   <u>a</u><u>b</u>   <u>monte.</u>

Lesson XIV

Go over these every day for 10 minutes.

VERBS

laudare	to praise	monēre	to warn
audire	to hear	agere	to act, to do
bibere	to drink	edere	to eat
vivere	to live	ponere	to put, to place
regere	to rule	vincere	to conquer
credere	to believe	ducere	to lead
currere	to run	mittere	to send
defendere	to defend	scribere	to write
sentire	to feel	munire	to build
dicere	to say	petere	to seek

NOUNS

dolor, doloris	pain, sorrow	panis, panis (m)	bread
mons, montis (m)	mountain	crux, crucis	cross
homo, hominis (m)	man	urbs, urbis	city
flumen, fluminis	river	civitas, civitatis	state
pax, pacis	peace	caput, capitis	head
Caesar, Caesaris	Caesar	Cicero, Ciceronis (m)	Cicero
canis, canis (m/f)	dog	veritas, veritatis	truth
virgo, virginis	virgin	arbor, arboris (f)	tree
sol, solis (m)	sun	rex, regis (m)	king
tempus, temporis (n)	time	civis, civis (m/f)	citizen
dux, ducis (m)	leader	lux, lucis	light
lex, legis	law	gens, gentis	tribe
fons, fontis (m)	fountain	tentatio, tentationis	temptation
caritas, caritatis	love	libertas, libertatis	freedom, liberty
pastor, pastoris	shepherd	mare, maris	sea

SPECIAL INDECLINABLE* WORDS:

non	not	diu	for a long time
saepe	often	bene	well
in (ablative)	in, on	in (accusative)	into, onto
ad (accusative)	to, towards	trans (accusative)	across
per (accusative)	through	contra (accusative)	against
ante (accusative)	before	post (accusative)	after
a, ab (ablative)	by	cum (ablative)	with
de (ablative)	from	e, ex (ablative)	out of

Indeclinable means they never change. They never change even an ending.

-o, or -m	I	-mus	we
-s	you (sing)	-tis	you
-t	he, she or it	-nt	they

sum, es, est, sumus, estis, sunt *(I am, you are, he is, we are, you are, they are)*

eram, eras, erat, eramus, eratis, erant *(I was, you were, he was, we were, you were, they were)*

ero, eris, erit, erimus, eritis, erunt *(I will be, you will be, he will be, we will be, you will be, they will be)*

possum, potes, potest, possumus, potestis, possunt *(I am able, you are able, he is able, we are able, you are able, they are able)*

poteram, poteras, poterat, poteramus, poteratis, poterant *(I was able, you were able, he was able, we were able, you were able, they were able)*

potero, poteris, poterit, poterimus, poteritis, poterunt *(I will be able, you will be able, he will be able, we will be able, you will be able, they will be able)*

volo, vis, vult, volumus, vultis, volunt *(I am willing, you are willing, he is willing, we are willing, you are willing, they are willing)*

nolo, non vis, non vult, nolumus, non vultis, nolunt *(I am not willing, you are not willing, he is not willing, we are not willing, you are not willing, they are not willing)*

malo, mavis, mavult, malumus, mavultis, malunt *(I prefer, you prefer, he prefers, we prefer, you prefer, they prefer) (Prefer means "to be more willing")*

Remember your rules for gender:

> **Feminine nouns usually end in s-o-x**
>
> **Neuter nouns usually end in l-a-n-c-e-t**
>
> **Masculine nouns end in er-r-or**
>
> **Words that clearly denote a person of a particular gender are in that gender.**
>
> **(Ex: Cicero is masculine)**

Remember the Latin names for English cases and how to get them:

> **Nominative = Subject = First Form**
>
> **Genitive = Possessive ('s or the object of "of") = Second Form**
>
> **Dative = Indirect Object (object of "for") = Stem + i**
>
> **Accusative = Direct Object or Object of some prepositions = Stem + em**
>
> **Ablative = Object of some prepositions = Stem + e**

Day 1, Exercise 1: Let's review our questions to ask to discover the cases.

Word Bank: a) 's   b) ablative   c) for   d) accusative

e) of   f) who or what   g) whom or what   h) for what purpose

1. To find the subject/nominative of a sentence ask yourself **_f) who or what_** did the action of the verb?

2. To find the direct object/accusative of a sentence ask yourself **_g) whom or what_ about the verb. Only do this AFTER locating the subject and verb.**

3. To find the possessive/genitive in a sentence look for either of these: an **_a) 's_** or the preposition **_e) of_**.

4. To find the indirect object/dative in a sentence look for any of these: the answer to the question "for whom" or **_h) for what purpose_** or the preposition **_c) for_**.

5. Prepositions other than "of" or "for" seem to take the **_d) accusative_** or the **_b) ablative_** case.

Day 1, Exercise 2: The nominative/subjects are circled and the genitive/possessives are boxed, the accusative/direct objects are underlined, and the datives/indirect objects (objects of for) are dash underlined.

Now, you need to put parentheses around prepositions and their objects and label the prepositions with a "p". Also, make sure to underline the objects of accusative prepositions.

Before doing this exercises let's go over this in more detail.

Look at your list of prepositions in the vocabulary section.

First, put "p" above the prepositions you find in the below sentences. (See my "p" above "through" and "by" in the example sentence.)

Next find the object of the prepositions. It's the next real word. Make sure you put the parentheses around the whole phrase. See below. I found the object of "through" which was "road". I put a set of parentheses around "through the road". I crossed out "the", of course. I did the same things for "by" the "house". ("House" is the object of "by".)

Finally, look to see if those prepositions took the accusative or the ablative. In my example, I saw that "through" took an accusative object. I saw that "by" took an ablative object. So, I underlined the object of "through" but not the object of "by".

Why do you think I underlined the object when it was accusative, but not ablative? Look at the word "road" below. Notice I underlined it with a single underline. I also use single underlines for accusative/direct objects.

I use single underlines for accusative/direct objects and accusative/objects of prepositions. I use a single underline for all accusatives.

Example: ~~The~~ man's (cat) ran (^p through ~~the~~ road)(^p by ~~the~~ house).

(This exercise is continued on the next page.)

Now you do some:

1. (He) begged for p<u>eace</u> (from Caesar.)

2. (Sophie) sent ~~the~~ <u>dog</u> (by ~~the~~ <u>city</u>) (~~to~~ <u>Caesar</u>.)

3. ~~The~~ (cross) was carried (across ~~the~~ <u>city</u>.)

Day 2, Exercise 1: Let's write all the cases of Latin nouns that we know in order.

Example: lex, legis

Nominative = Subject = First Form =	**<u>lex</u>**
Genitive = Possessive = Second Form =	**<u>legis</u>**
Dative = Indirect Object = Stem + i =	**<u>legi</u>**
Accusative = Direct Object/Obj of Prepositions = Stem + em =	**<u>legem</u>**
Ablative = Obj of Prepositions = Stem + e =	**<u>lege</u>**

A. sol, solis

Nominative = Subject = First Form =	**<u>sol</u>**
Genitive = Possessive = Second Form =	**<u>solis</u>**
Dative = Indirect Object = Stem + i =	**<u>soli</u>**
Accusative = Direct Object/Obj of Prepositions = Stem + em =	**<u>solem</u>**
Ablative = Obj of Prepositions = Stem + e =	**<u>sole</u>**

(This exercise is continued on the next page.)

B. panis, panis

Nominative = Subject = First Form = **_panis_**

Genitive = Possessive = Second Form = **_panis_**

Dative = Indirect Object = Stem + i = **_pani_**

Accusative = Direct Object/Obj of Prepositions = Stem + em = **_panem_**

Ablative = Obj of Prepositions = Stem + e = **_pane_**

C. civitas, civitatis

Nominative = Subject = First Form = **_civitas_**

Genitive = Possessive = Second Form = **_civitatis_**

Dative = Indirect Object = Stem + i = **_civitati_**

Accusative = Direct Object/Obj of Prepositions = Stem + em = **_civitatem_**

Ablative = Obj of Prepositions = Stem + e = **_civitate_**

D. urbs, urbis

Nominative = Subject = First Form = **_urbs_**

Genitive = Possessive = Second Form = **_urbis_**

Dative = Indirect Object = Stem + i = **_urbi_**

Accusative = Direct Object/Obj of Prepositions = Stem + em = **_urbem_**

Ablative = Obj of Prepositions = Stem + e = **_urbe_**

Day 2, Exercise 2: Do a complete synopsis of the verb 'scribere'. The following chart will help.

3rd Present	4th Present	3rd Past	4th Past
rego	audio	regebam	audiebam
regis	audis	regebas	audiebas
regit	audit	regebat	audiebat
regimus	audimus	regebamus	audiebamus
regitis	auditis	regebatis	audiebatis
regunt	audiunt	regebant	audiebant

3rd Future Regular	4th Future Regular	3rd Future Possibles	4th Future Possibles
regam	audiam	regam	audiam
reges	audies	regas	audias
reget	audiet	regat	audiat
regemus	audiemus	regamus	audiamus
regetis	audietis	regatis	audiatis
regent	audient	regant	audiant

> **A verb that loves its i will keep it, but otherwise it copycats the -ere verbs. It doesn't have to change the "e" to "i" for the present, because it is already an "i." However, it adds the "e" for the past and future, so it can be just like the third conjugation -ere words, but it doesn't lose its "i." It loves its "i." The future possible changes the "e" of the regular to an "a."**

(This exercise is continued on the next page.)

	Present	Past	Future Regulars	Future Possibles
1st Singular	*scribo*	*scribebam*	*scribam*	*scribam*
2nd Singular	*scribis*	*scribebas*	*scribes*	*scribas*
3rd Singular	*scribit*	*scribebat*	*scribet*	*scribat*
1st Plural	*scribimus*	*scribebamus*	*scribemus*	*scribamus*
2nd Plural	*scribitis*	*scribebatis*	*scribetis*	*scribatis*
3rd Plural	*scribunt*	*scribebant*	*scribent*	*scribant*

Day 3, Exercise 1: Fill in the chart:

Latin Prepositions that take the Accusative Case	Latin Prepositions that take the Ablative Case
ad	in
per	a, ab
ante	de
in	cum
trans	e, ex
contra	
post	

Day 3, Exercise 2: Translate following these steps:

> Step 1: Please circle the subject, box the possessives and underline the <u>direct objects</u>. Use a dashed line under the indirect object. Cross out the words, "the," "a," or "an."
>
> Step 2: Write the Latin word you would use on Line A above the word. Remember that there is no Latin word for "of," "for," "the," "a," or "an."
>
> Step 3: Write the stem of the words (which need the stem form) on line B.
>
> Step 4: Add the correct endings to complete the translation on line C.

Now let's apply these steps to the first sentence below: <u>*The man will believe Caesar's law for Cicero.*</u>

> Step 1: Please circle the subject, box the possessives and underline the direct objects. Cross out the words, "the," "a," or "an."

a) Locate the verb. It has a shaded box below it. So in this sentence it is "will believe".

b) Ask yourself "Who/what will believe?" Answer: Man. "Man" is the subject; circle it.

c) The man will believe whom/what? Answer: Law. "Law" is the direct object; underline it.

d) Are there any possessives? These words have 's in them or they are the object of "of." Answer: Yes, Caesar is the possessive. Box Caesar's.

e) Ask yourself "The man will believe law for whom/what purpose?" Answer: Cicero. "Cicero" is the indirect object. Dash underline under the word Cicero.

f) Now, cross out any "the," "a," or "an"s. So, cross out the word "the" in this sentence.

> **Step 2: Write the Latin word you would use on Line A above the word. Remember that there is no Latin word for "the," "a," or "an."**

On line "A", write the words as they appear in your vocabulary. Put "NA" for any words that are not translated. So, you would have:

The = NA (line A)

man = homo, hominis (line A)

will believe = credere (line A)

Caesar's = Caesar, Caesaris (line A)

law = lex, legis (line A)

for = NA (line A)

Cicero = Cicero, Ciceronis (line A)

> **Step 3: Write the stem of the words (which need the stem form) on line B.**

You only have to write the stem for words that need the stem to build the word. So, in this case put the stem down for credere (crede) and lex, legis (leg-) and Cicero, Ciceronis (Ciceron-).

> **Step 4: Add the correct endings to complete the translation on line C.**

The correct form of "homo, hominis" is the first form, which is the nominative form used for the subject. So it is **homo**.

The correct form of "Caesar, Caesaris" is the second form, which is the genitive form used for the possessive. So it is **Caesaris.**

The correct form of "lex, legis" is the stem + em, which is the accusative form used for the direct object. So it is **legem.**

(This exercise is continued on the next page.)

The correct form of "Cicero, Ciceronis" is the stem + i, which is the dative form used for the indirect object. So it is **Ciceroni.**

The shaded box reminds you this is a verb word so think about these things when you translate that word.

a) What is the tense? ***Answer: future.***

b) What do you do to the stem because of that tense? for example, change e to i to get the present for an -ere word.) ***Answer: Leave it alone.***

c) What personal ending do you use. (In other words is "man" an "I," "you," "he," "she," or "it.") Plug in your word in the shaded box. ***Answer: "t" for "he." Word is "credet."***

1.

A.	*NA*	*pastor, pastoris*	*edere*	*panis, panis*	*ante*	*Caesar, Caesaris*
B.			*ede*	*pan*	(Accusative)	*Caesar*
	The shepherd		may eat	bread	(before | Caesar.)
C.		*Pastor*	*edat*	*panem*	*ante*	*Caesarem.*

2.

A.	*Cicero, Ciceronis*	*defendere*	*contra*	*Caesar, Caesaris*
B.		*defende*	(Accusative)	*Caesar*
	Cicero	will defend	(against	Caesar.)
C.	*Cicero*	*defendet*	*contra*	*Caesarem.*

Lesson XV

Go over these every day for 10 minutes.

VERBS

laudare	to praise	monēre	to warn
audire	to hear	agere	to act, to do
bibere	to drink	edere	to eat
vivere	to live	ponere	to put, to place
regere	to rule	vincere	to conquer
credere	to believe	ducere	to lead
currere	to run	mittere	to send
defendere	to defend	scribere	to write
sentire	to feel	munire	to build
dicere	to say	petere	to seek
trahere	**to draw**	**gerere**	**to conduct, wage**
discere	**to learn**		

NOUNS

dolor, doloris	pain, sorrow	panis, panis (m)	bread
mons, montis (m)	mountain	crux, crucis	cross
homo, hominis (m)	man	urbs, urbis	city
flumen, fluminis	river	civitas, civitatis	state
pax, pacis	peace	caput, capitis	head
Caesar, Caesaris	Caesar	Cicero, Ciceronis (m)	Cicero
canis, canis (m/f)	dog	veritas, veritatis	truth
virgo, virginis	virgin	arbor, arboris (f)	tree
sol, solis (m)	sun	rex, regis (m)	king
tempus, temporis (n)	time	civis, civis (m/f)	citizen
dux, ducis (m)	leader	lux, lucis	light
lex, legis	law	gens, gentis	tribe
fons, fontis (m)	fountain	tentatio, tentationis	temptation
caritas, caritatis	love	libertas, libertatis	freedom, liberty
pastor, pastoris	shepherd	mare, maris	sea

Special indeclinable* words:

non	not	diu	for a long time
saepe	often	bene	well
in (ablative)	in, on	in (accusative)	into, onto
ad (accusative)	to, towards	trans (accusative)	across
per (accusative)	through	contra (accusative)	against
ante (accusative)	before	post (accusative)	after
a, ab (ablative)	by	cum (ablative)	with
de (ablative)	from	e, ex (ablative)	out of

* Indeclinable means they never change. They never change even an ending.

-o, or -m	I	-mus	we
-s	you (sing)	-tis	you
-t	he, she, or it	-nt	they

sum, es, est, sumus, estis, sunt *(I am, you are, he is, we are, you are, they are)*

eram, eras, erat, eramus, eratis, erant *(I was, you were, he was, we were, you were, they were)*

ero, eris, erit, erimus, eritis, erunt *(I will be, you will be, he will be, we will be, you will be, they will be)*

possum, potes, potest, possumus, potestis, possunt *(I am able, you are able, he is able, we are able, you are able, they are able)*

poteram, poteras, poterat, poteramus, poteratis, poterant *(I was able, you were able, he was able, we were able, you were able, they were able)*

potero, poteris, poterit, poterimus, poteritis, poterunt *(I will be able, you will be able, he will be able, we will be able, you will be able, they will be able)*

volo, vis, vult, volumus, vultis, volunt *(I am willing, you are willing, he is willing, we are willing, you are willing, they are willing)*

nolo, non vis, non vult, nolumus, non vultis, nolunt *(I am not willing, you are not willing, he is not willing, we are not willing, you are not willing, they are not willing)*

malo, mavis, mavult, malumus, mavultis, malunt *(I prefer, you prefer, he prefers, we prefer, you prefer, they prefer) (Prefer means "to be more willing")*

Remember your rules for gender:

> **Feminine nouns usually end in s-o-x**
>
> **Neuter nouns usually end in l-a-n-c-e-t**
>
> **Masculine nouns end in er-r-or**
>
> **Words that clearly denote a person of a particular gender are in that gender.**
> **(Ex: Cicero is masculine)**

Remember the Latin names for English cases and how to get them:

> **Nominative = Subject = First Form**
>
> **Genitive = Possessive ('s or the object of "of") = Second Form**
>
> **Dative = Indirect Object (object of "for") = Stem + i**
>
> **Accusative = Direct Object or Object of some prepositions = Stem + em**
>
> **Ablative = Object of some prepositions = Stem + e**

Neuter nouns have a different accusative ending. The neuter accusative is always the same as the neuter nominative.

> **Accusative MASCULINE AND FEMININE = Direct Object or Object of some prepositions = Stem + em**
>
> **Accusative NEUTER = Same as Nominative**

Day 1, Exercise 1: Give the accusative of the following words:

flumen, fluminis	*flumen*
caput, capitis	*caput*
tempus, temporis	*tempus*
sol, solis	*solem*
arbor, arboris	*arborem*
caritas, caritatis	*caritatem*

Day 1, Exercise 2: Circle the nominative/subjects, box the genitive/possessives, underline the accusative/direct objects, and dash underline the datives/indirect objects (objects of for). Put parentheses around prepositions and their objects and label the prepositions with a "p". Also, make sure to underline the objects of accusative prepositions.

Before doing this exercises let's go over this in more detail.

Look at your list of prepositions in the vocabulary section.

First, put "p" above the prepositions you find in the below sentences. (See my "p" above "through" and "by" in the example sentence.)

Next find the object of the prepositions. It's the next real word. Make sure you put the parentheses around the whole phrase. See below. I found the object of "through" which was "road". I put a set of parentheses around "through the road". I crossed out "the", of course. I did the same things for "by" the "house". ("House" is the object of "by".)

Finally, look at the vocabulary list to see if those prepositions took the accusative or the ablative. In my example, I saw that "through" took an accusative object. I saw that "by" took an ablative object. So, I underlined the object of "through" but not the object of "by".

Did you notice that I underlined the object when it was accusative, but not ablative? Look at the word "road" below. Notice I underlined it with a single underline. I also use single underlines for accusative/direct objects.

I use single underlines for accusative/direct objects and accusative/objects of prepositions. I use a single underline for all accusatives.

Example: The man's cat ran (through the road)(by the house).

Here are your sentences:

1. The ship sailed (across the sea).

2. The neighbor's dog chases the cat of the neighbor.

3. Sir Percival ran (into a bank).

4. Sir Percival ran (in a bank).

5. Mary came (with Teresa's family).

Note - In #2, 'of the neighbor' could also be boxed.

Day 2, Exercise 1: Let's write all the cases of Latin nouns that we know in order.

Example: lex, legis

Nominative = Subject = First Form =	lex
Genitive = Possessive = Second Form =	legis
Dative = Indirect Object = Stem + i =	legi
Accusative = D.O./O. P. = (M/F) Stem + em OR (N) Nominative =	legem
Ablative = Obj of Prepositions = Stem + e =	lege

A. flumen, fluminis

Nominative = Subject = First Form =	*flumen*
Genitive = Possessive = Second Form =	*fluminis*
Dative = Indirect Object = Stem + i =	*flumini*
Accusative = D.O./O. P. = (M/F) Stem + em OR (N) Same as Nom =	*flumen**
Ablative = Obj of Prepositions = Stem + e =	*flumine*

B. caput, capitis

Nominative = Subject = First Form =	*caput*
Genitive = Possessive = Second Form =	*capitis*
Dative = Indirect Object = Stem + i =	*capiti*
Accusative = D.O./O. P. = (M/F) Stem + em OR (N) Same as Nom =	*caput**
Ablative = Obj of Prepositions = Stem + e =	*capite*

* This word is a neuter, so its Accusative is the same as its Nominative.

(This exercise is continued on the next page.)

C. dolor, doloris

Nominative = Subject = First Form =　　　　　　　　　　　　*dolor*

Genitive = Possessive = Second Form =　　　　　　　　　　　*doloris*

Dative = Indirect Object = Stem + i =　　　　　　　　　　　　*dolori*

Accusative = D.O./O. P. = (M/F) Stem + em OR (N) Same as Nom =　*dolorem*

Ablative = Obj of Prepositions = Stem + e =　　　　　　　　　*dolore*

D. tempus, temporis

Nominative = Subject = First Form =　　　　　　　　　　　　*tempus*

Genitive = Possessive = Second Form =　　　　　　　　　　　*temporis*

Dative = Indirect Object = Stem + i =　　　　　　　　　　　　*tempori*

Accusative = D.O./O. P. = (M/F) Stem + em OR (N) Same as Nom =　*tempus**

Ablative = Obj of Prepositions = Stem + e =　　　　　　　　　*tempore*

* This word is a neuter, so its Accusative is the same as its Nominative.

Day 2, Exercise 2: Do a complete synopsis of the verb 'gerere'.

A verb that loves its i will keep it, but otherwise it copycats the -ere verbs. It doesn't have to change the "e" to "i" for the present, because it is already an "i". However, it adds the "e" for the past and future, so it can be just like the third conjugation -ere words, but it doesn't lose its "i". It loves its "i". The future possible changes the "e" of the regular to an "a".

	Present	Past	Future Regulars	Future Possibles
1st Singular	gero	gerebam	geram	geram
2nd Singular	geris	gerebas	geres	geras
3rd Singular	gerit	gerebat	geret	gerat
1st Plural	gerimus	gerebamus	geremus	geramus
2nd Plural	geritis	gerebatis	geretis	geratis
3rd Plural	gerunt	gerebant	gerent	gerant

The i-stem nouns.

We are going to be working on a few new noun endings. To do this we need to split our nouns into two groups: those that are regular and those that are i-stem. A noun is considered i-stem if it either:

a) **Ends in -is or -es in the nominative first form and has the same number of syllables in the first and second form.**

b) **Ends in -s or -x in the nominative first form and has a stem that ends in two consonants.**

c) **Ends in -al, -ar, or -e in the nominative first form (neuter nouns).**

Day 3, Exercise 1: Say whether the following nouns are regular or i-stem.

lux, lucis	_regular_
caput, capitis	_regular_
tempus, temporis	_regular_
sol, solis	_regular_
panis, panis	_i-stem_
caritas, caritatis	_regular_

Day 3, Exercise 2: Translate following these steps:

Step 1: Please circle the subject, box the possessives and underline the <u>direct objects</u>. Use a dashed line under the indirect object. Cross out the words, "the", "a", or "an". Put parentheses (around prepositional phrases using accusatives or ablatives). Make sure you write "p" above the preposition and <u>underline</u> the object of the preposition once if it is accusative and do nothing if the object is ablative.

Step 2: Write the Latin word you would use on Line A above the word. Remember that there is no Latin word for "of", "for", "the","a" or "an".

Step 3: Write the stem of the words (which need the stem form) on line B.

Step 4: Add the correct endings to complete the translation on line C.

1.

A. <u>**NA**</u>   <u>*urbs, urbis*</u>   <u>*discere*</u>   <u>*veritas, veritatis*</u>   <u>*per*</u>   <u>*Caesar, Caesaris*</u>

B.   <u>*disce*</u>   <u>*veritat*</u>   *(Accusative)*   <u>**Caesar**</u>

   The   (city)   learns   <u>truth</u>   (through   <u>Caesar.</u>)

C.   <u>*Urbs*</u>   *discit*   <u>*veritatem*</u>   <u>*per*</u>   <u>*Caesarem.*</u>

(This exercise is continued on the next page.)

2.

A. **<u>Caesar, Caesaris</u>**   <u>petere</u>   <u>pax, pacis</u>   <u>trans</u>   <u>NA</u>   <u>mare</u>

B. <u>pete</u>   <u>pac</u>   *(Accusative)*   <u>mar</u>

(Caesar)   was seeking   <u>peace</u>   (across   the   <u>sea</u>*.)

C. **<u>Caesar</u>**   <u>petebat</u>   <u>pacem</u>   <u>trans</u>   <u>mare.</u>

*Remember "sea" is a neuter word, so its accusative is the same as the nominative.

134

Lesson XVI

Go over these every day for 10 minutes. New words are in bold.

VERBS

laudare	to praise	monēre	to warn
audire	to hear	agere	to act, to do
bibere	to drink	edere	to eat
vivere	to live	ponere	to put, to place
regere	to rule	vincere	to conquer
credere	to believe	ducere	to lead
currere	to run	mittere	to send
defendere	to defend	scribere	to write
sentire	to feel	munire	to build
dicere	to say	petere	to seek
trahere	**to draw**	**gerere**	**to conduct, wage**
discere	**to learn**	**cedere**	**to yield**

NOUNS

dolor, doloris	pain, sorrow	panis, panis (m)	bread
mons, montis (m)	mountain	crux, crucis	cross
homo, hominis (m)	man	urbs, urbis	city
flumen, fluminis	river	civitas, civitatis	state
pax, pacis	peace	caput, capitis	head
Caesar, Caesaris	Caesar	Cicero, Ciceronis (m)	Cicero
canis, canis (m/f)	dog	veritas, veritatis	truth
virgo, virginis	virgin	arbor, arboris (f)	tree
sol, solis (m)	sun	rex, regis (m)	king
tempus, temporis (n)	time	civis, civis (m/f)	citizen
dux, ducis (m)	leader	lux, lucis	light
lex, legis	law	gens, gentis	tribe
fons, fontis (m)	fountain	tentatio, tentationis	temptation
caritas, caritatis	love	libertas, libertatis	freedom, liberty
pastor, pastoris	shepherd	mare, maris	sea

Beginning Latin II - Lesson XVI

SPECIAL INDECLINABLE* WORDS:

non	not	diu	for a long time
saepe	often	bene	well
in (ablative)	in, on	in (accusative)	into, onto
ad (accusative)	to, towards	trans (accusative)	across
per (accusative)	through	contra (accusative)	against
ante (accusative)	before	post (accusative)	after
a, ab (ablative)	by	cum (ablative)	with
de (ablative)	from, **down from**	e, ex (ablative)	out of

* Indeclinable means they never change. They never change even an ending.

-o, or -m	I	-mus	we
-s	you (sing)	-tis	you
-t	he, she, or it	-nt	they

sum, es, est, sumus, estis, sunt *(I am, you are, he is, we are, you are, they are)*

eram, eras, erat, eramus, eratis, erant *(I was, you were, he was, we were, you were, they were)*

ero, eris, erit, erimus, eritis, erunt *(I will be, you will be, he will be, we will be, you will be, they will be)*

possum, potes, potest, possumus, potestis, possunt *(I am able, you are able, he is able, we are able, you are able, they are able)*

poteram, poteras, poterat, poteramus, poteratis, poterant *(I was able, you were able, he was able, we were able, you were able, they were able)*

potero, poteris, poterit, poterimus, poteritis, poterunt *(I will be able, you will be able, he will be able, we will be able, you will be able, they will be able)*

volo, vis, vult, volumus, vultis, volunt *(I am willing, you are willing, he is willing, we are willing, you are willing, they are willing)*

nolo, non vis, non vult, nolumus, non vultis, nolunt *(I am not willing, you are not willing, he is not willing, we are not willing, you are not willing, they are not willing)*

malo, mavis, mavult, malumus, mavultis, malunt *(I prefer, you prefer, he prefers, we prefer, you prefer, they prefer) (Prefer means "to be more willing")*

fero, fers, fert, ferimus, fertis, ferunt *(I bear, you bear, he bears, we bear, you bear, they bear)**

*Just memorize this word and its meanings for now.

Remember your rules for gender:

> **Feminine nouns usually end in s-o-x**
>
> **Neuter nouns usually end in l-a-n-c-e-t**
>
> **Masculine nouns end in er-r-or**
>
> **Words that clearly denote a person of a particular gender are in that gender.**
> **(Ex: Cicero is masculine)**

Remember the Latin names for English cases and how to get them:

> **Nominative = Subject = First Form**
>
> **Genitive = Possessive ('s or the object of "of") = Second Form**
>
> **Dative = Indirect Object (object of "for") = Stem + i**
>
> **Accusative MASCULINE AND FEMININE = Direct Object or Object of some prepositions**
> **= Stem + em**
>
> **Accusative NEUTER = Direct Object or Object of some prepositions = Same as Nominative**
>
> **Ablative = Object of some prepositions = Stem + e**

As you probably noticed in the box above, I added some more information about finding accusatives. Neuter accusatives are different than masculine and feminine accusatives. How do we know if a noun is masculine, feminine, or neuter? Remember our rules:

> **Feminine nouns usually end in s-o-x**
>
> **Neuter nouns usually end in l-a-n-c-e-t**
>
> **Masculine nouns end in er-r-or**
>
> **Words that clearly denote a person of a particular gender are in that gender.**
> **(Ex: Cicero is masculine)**

Don't forget that there are some exceptions to these rules that are marked in the vocabulary. You should have these exceptions memorized.

After we know what the gender of our noun is, we can then make the accusative. If the noun is masculine or feminine, then we find the accusative by doing stem + em, just like before. But if the noun is neuter, then the accusative is the same as the nominative.

(This exercise is continued on the next page.)

Examples:

Pastor, pastoris. What is its gender? Masculine, because the nominative/first form ends in "or." So, what is the accusative? The rule is stem + em. What is the stem? pastor. So the accusative of pastor, pastoris is pastorem.

Flumen, fluminis. What is its gender? Neuter, because the nominative/first form ends in "n." So, what is the accusative? The rule is same as nominative. What is the nominative? Flumen. So the accusative of flumen, fluminis is flumen.

Practice this in the following exercise:

Day 1, Exercise 1: Give the accusative of the following words:

Remember: Neuter nouns have a different accusative ending. The neuter accusative is always the same as the neuter nominative.

pastor, pastoris	***pastorem***
canis, canis	***canem***
tempus, temporis	***tempus****
flumen, fluminis	***flumen***
mare, maris	***mare***
caput, capitis	***caput***

* The student should remember from the vocabulary that this is an irregular verb. It follows the rules for a feminine noun, but is actually neuter.

Day 1, Exercise 2: Circle the nominative/subjects, box the genitive/possessives, underline the accusative/direct objects, and dash underline the datives/ indirect objects (objects of for). Put parentheses around prepositions and their objects and label the prepositions with a "p". Also, make sure to underline the objects of accusative prepositions.

(This exercise is continued on the next page.)

Before doing this exercises let's go over this in more detail.

Look at your list of prepositions in the vocabulary section.

First, put "p" above the prepositions you find in the below sentences. (See my "p" above "through" and "by" in the example sentence.)

Next find the object of the prepositions. It's the next real word. Make sure you put the parentheses around the whole phrase. See below. I found the object of "through" which was "road". I put a set of parentheses around "through the road". I crossed out "the", of course. I did the same things for "by" the "house". ("House" is the object of "by".)

Finally, look at the vocabulary list to see if those prepositions took the accusative or the ablative. In my example, I saw that "through" took an accusative object. I saw that "by" took an ablative object. So, I underlined the object of "through" but not the object of "by".

Did you notice that I underlined the object when it was accusative, but not ablative? Look at the word "road" below. Notice I underlined it with a single underline. I also use single underlines for accusative/direct objects.

I use single underlines for accusative/direct objects and accusative/objects of prepositions. I use a single underline for all accusatives.

Example: ~~The~~ man's (cat) ran (through ~~the~~ road)(by ~~the~~ house).

Here are your sentences:

1. The (car) raced (through the sand.)

2. Jill's (cat) looks (down from the tree.)

3. (Caesar) ate a salad of greens* (before the battle.)

4. (Peter) hit the ball (towards the pitcher.)

5. (Mary) looked (through the window.)

* The student may or may not put parenthesis around "of" possessives and "for" indirect objects. Either way is acceptable. These are prepositional phrases, but they are treated differently than "normal" prepositions. In this answer key they will not be marked.

༄ Beginning Latin II - Lesson XVI ༅

Day 2, Exercise 1: Let's write all the cases of Latin nouns that we know in order.

Example: lex, legis

Nominative = Subject = First Form =   *__lex__*

Genitive = Possessive = Second Form =   *__legis__*

Dative = Indirect Object = Stem + i =   *__legi__*

Accusative = D.O./O. P. = (M/F) Stem + em OR (N) Nominative =   *__legem__*

Ablative = Obj of Prepositions = Stem + e =   *__lege__*

A. tempus, temporis

Nominative = Subject = First Form =   *__tempus__*

Genitive = Possessive = Second Form =   *__temporis__*

Dative = Indirect Object = Stem + i =   *__tempori__*

Accusative = D.O./O. P. = (M/F) Stem + em OR (N) Same as Nom =   *__tempus__***

Ablative = Obj of Prepositions = Stem + e =   *__tempore__*

B. sol, solis

Nominative = Subject = First Form =   *__sol__*

Genitive = Possessive = Second Form =   *__solis__*

Dative = Indirect Object = Stem + i =   *__soli__*

Accusative = D.O./O. P. = (M/F) Stem + em OR (N) Same as Nom =   *__solem__***

Ablative = Obj of Prepositions = Stem + e =   *__sole__*

(This exercise is continued on the next page.)

C. dux, ducis

Nominative = Subject = First Form =   **_dux_**

Genitive = Possessive = Second Form =   **_ducis_**

Dative = Indirect Object = Stem + i =   **_duci_**

Accusative = D.O./O. P. = (M/F) Stem + em OR (N) Same as Nom =   **_ducem_**

Ablative = Obj of Prepositions = Stem + e =   **_duce_**

D. mare, maris

Nominative = Subject = First Form =   **_mare_**

Genitive = Possessive = Second Form =   **_maris_**

Dative = Indirect Object = Stem + i =   **_mari_**

Accusative = D.O/O.P = (M/F) Stem +em OR (N) Same as Nom =   **_mare_**

Ablative = Obj of Prepositions = Stem + e =   **_mari*_**

*This ending is the ablative ending for neuter i-stems. We will learn it later.

** *These words are irregulars.*

Day 2, Exercise 2: Do a complete synopsis of the verb 'cedere'.

A verb that loves its i will keep it, but otherwise it copycats the -ere verbs. It doesn't have to change the "e" to "i" for the present, because it is already an "i." However, it adds the "e" for the past and future, so it can be just like the third conjugation -ere words, but it doesn't lose its "i." It loves its "i." The future possible changes the "e" of the regular to an "a."

	Present	Past	Future Regulars	Future Possibles
1st Singular	cedo	cedebam	cedam	cedam
2nd Singular	cedis	cedebas	cedes	cedas
3rd Singular	cedit	cedebat	cedet	cedat
1st Plural	cedimus	cedebamus	cedemus	cedamus
2nd Plural	ceditis	cedebatis	cedetis	cedatis
3rd Plural	cedunt	cedebant	cedent	cedant

Now we are going to learn about i-stem nouns. Here are the rules for i-stem nouns:

A noun is i - stem if it.....

Ends in -is or -es in the nominative first form and has the same number of syllables in the first and second form.

Ends in -s or -x in the nominative first form and has a stem that ends in two consonants.

Ends in -al, -ar, or -e in the nominative first form (neuter nouns).

Day 3, Exercise 1: Say whether the following nouns are regular or i-stem.

As you saw today, in Exercise 3, i-stem nouns have an "i" not an "e" in the neuter ablative singular. You have only one neuter i-stem noun in the vocabulary list. What is it?

__mare, maris__

Put an "x" next to each noun that is i-stem.

___ dolor, doloris	pain, sorrow		_x_ panis, panis (m)	bread
_x_ mons, montis (m)	mountain		___ crux, crucis	cross
___ homo, hominis (m)	man		_x_ urbs, urbis	city
___ flumen, fluminis	river		___ civitas, civitatis	state
___ pax, pacis	peace		___ caput, capitis	head
___ Caesar, Caesaris	Caesar		___ Cicero, Ciceronis (m)	Cicero
_x_ canis, canis (m/f)	dog		___ veritas, veritatis	truth
___ virgo, virginis	virgin		___ arbor, arboris (f)	tree
___ sol, solis (m)	sun		___ rex, regis (m)	king
___ tempus, temporis (n)	time		_x_ civis, civis (m/f)	citizen
___ dux, ducis (m)	leader		___ lux, lucis	light
___ lex, legis	law		_x_ gens, gentis	tribe
_x_ fons, fontis (m)	fountain		___ tentatio, tentationis	temptation
___ caritas, caritatis	love		___ libertas, libertatis	freedom, liberty
___ pastor, pastoris	shepherd		_x_ mare, maris	sea

Day 3, Exercise 2: Translate following these steps:

> Step 1: Please circle the subject, box the possessives and underline the direct objects. Use a dashed line under the indirect object. Cross out the words, "the," "a," or "an." Put parentheses (around prepositional phrases using accusatives or ablatives). Make sure you write "p" above the preposition and underline the object of the preposition once if it is accusative and do nothing if the object is ablative.
>
> Step 2: Write the Latin word you would use on Line A above the word. Remember that there is no Latin word for "of," "for," "the," "a," or "an".
>
> Step 3: Write the stem of the words (which need the stem form) on line B.
>
> Step 4: Add the correct endings to complete the translation on line C.

1.

A. *NA*	*civitas, civitatis*	*audire*	*veritas, veritatis*	*de*	*Cicero, Ciceronis*
B.		*audi*	*veritat*	*(Ablative)*	*Ciceron*
	The (state)	hears	truth	(from	Cicero.)
C.	*Civitas*	*audit*	*veritatem*	*de*	*Cicerone.*

2.

A. *Caesar, Caesaris*	*mittere*	*NA*	*canis, canis*	*ad*	*NA*	*dux, ducis*
B.	*mitte*		*can*	*(Accusative)*		*duc*
(Caesar)	was sending	the	dog	(to	the	leader.)
C. *Caesar*	*mittebat*		*canem*	*ad*		*ducem.*

Review Lesson B

Day 1, Exercise 1: Do a complete synopsis of the verb "munire":

	Present	Past	Future Regulars	Future Possibles
1st Singular	*munio*	*muniebam*	*muniam*	*muniam*
2nd Singular	*munis*	*muniebas*	*munies*	*munias*
3rd Singular	*munit*	*muniebat*	*muniet*	*muniat*
1st Plural	*munimus*	*muniebamus*	*muniemus*	*muniamus*
2nd Plural	*munitis*	*muniebatis*	*munietis*	*muniatis*
3rd Plural	*muniunt*	*muniebant*	*munient*	*muniant*

Day 1, Exercise 2: True or False

laudare..................................to warn	True	***False***
monēre..................................to praise	True	***False***
audire..................................to hear	***True***	False
agere..................................to do	***True***	False
civitas, civitatis..................................state	***True***	False
pax, pacis..................................peace	***True***	False
caput, capitis..................................cross	True	***False***
Caesar, Caesaris..................................Caesar	***True***	False
diu..................................for a long time	***True***	False
lux, lucis..................................law	True	***False***

Day 1, Exercise 3: Do a complete synopsis of the verb "edere".

	Present	Past	Future Regulars	Future Possibles
1st Singular	edo	edebam	edam	edam
2nd Singular	edis	edebas	edes	edas
3rd Singular	edit	edebat	edet	edat
1st Plural	edimus	edebamus	edemus	edamus
2nd Plural	editis	edebatis	edetis	edatis
3rd Plural	edunt	edebant	edent	edant

Day 1, Exercise 4: Translate.

A. I may build. **muniam**

B. They will build. **munient**

C. He was building. **muniebat**

D. You (singular) build. **munis**

E. We were eating. **edebamus**

F. She will eat. **edet**

G. It may eat. **edat**

H. You (plural) eat. **editis**

Day 1, Exercise 5: Fill in the blanks:

	Word	Meaning
1st Singular	*malo*	I prefer
2nd Singular	*mavis*	you prefer
3rd Singular	*mavult*	he prefers
1st Plural	*malumus*	we prefer
2nd Plural	*mavultis*	you prefer
3rd Plural	*malunt*	they prefer

	Word	Meaning
1st Singular	*fero*	I bear
2nd Singular	*fers*	you bear
3rd Singular	*fert*	he bears
1st Plural	*ferimus*	we bear
2nd Plural	*fertis*	you bear
3rd Plural	*ferunt*	they bear

(This exercise is continued on the next page.)

	Word	Meaning
1st Singular	sum	*I am*
2nd Singular	es	*you are*
3rd Singular	est	*he is*
1st Plural	sumus	*we are*
2nd Plural	estis	*you are*
3rd Plural	sunt	*they are*

Day 1, Exercise 6: Find the stem of the following words:

audire <u>*audi*</u>

sol, solis <u>*sol*</u>

flumen, fluminis <u>*flumin*</u>

pastor, pastoris <u>*pastor*</u>

trahere <u>*trahe*</u>

gerere <u>*gere*</u>

tempus, temporis <u>*tempor*</u>

veritas, veritatis <u>*veritat*</u>

Day 2, Exercise 1: True or False

bibere..to drink <u>***True***</u> False

edere..to edit True <u>***False***</u>

vivere..to conquer True <u>***False***</u>

(This exercise is continued on the next page.)

ponere...to place		***True***	False
regere..to rule		***True***	False
non..for a long time		True	***False***
urbs, urbis..herb		True	***False***
flumen, fluminis....................................river		***True***	False
Cicero, Ciceronis (m)...........................Cicero		***True***	False
canis, canis (m/f..................................dog		***True***	False
veritas, veritatis....................................virgin		True	***False***
virgo, virginis..virgin		***True***	False

Day 2, Exercise 2: True or False

A noun is i-stem if it.....

Ends in -is or -es in the nominative first form and has the same number of syllables in the first and second form.	***True***	False
Ends in -s or -x in the nominative first form and has a stem that ends in two vowels.	True	***False***
Ends in -al, -ar, or -e in the nominative first form (masculine nouns).	True	***False***

Day 2, Exercise 3: Match the correct associations.

Nominative *(First Form)*   Stem + i

Accusative (neuter) *(Same as nominative)*   First Form

Dative *(Stem + i)*   Stem +e

Ablative *(Stem + e)*   Same as nominative

Accusative (masc or fem) *(Stem + em)*   Second Form

Genitive *(Second Form)*   Stem + em

Day 2, Exercise 4: Match the correct associations.

Subject *(Nominative)*	L-A-N-C-E-T
Possessive *(Genitive)*	ER-R-OR
3rd Person Plural *(They)*	Genitive
Feminine Words *(S-O-X)*	He, She, It
3rd Person Singular *(He, She, It)*	Accusative
Neuter Words *(L-A-N-C-E-T)*	Indirect Objects/Objects of "for"
2nd Person Singular *(You, sing)*	S-O-X
1st Person Singular *(I)*	They
Dative *(Indirect Objects/Objects of "for")*	You (sing)
Direct Objects *(Accusative)*	Nominative
Masculine Words *(ER-R-OR)*	We
1st Person Plural *(We)*	I

Day 2, Exercise 5: Fill in the blanks:

	Word	Meaning
1st Singular	*potero*	I will be able
2nd Singular	*poteris*	you will be able
3rd Singular	*poterit*	it will be able
1st Plural	*poterimus*	we will be able
2nd Plural	*poteritis*	you will be able
3rd Plural	*poterunt*	they will be able

(This exercise is continued on the next page.)

	Word	Meaning
1st Singular	nolo	*I am not willing*
2nd Singular	non vis	*you are not willing*
3rd Singular	non vult	*he is not willing*
1st Plural	nolumus	*we are not willing*
2nd Plural	non vultis	*you are not wiling*
3rd Plural	nolunt	*they are not willing*

	Word	Meaning
1st Singular	*volo*	I am willing
2nd Singular	*vis*	you are willing
3rd Singular	*vult*	he is willing
1st Plural	*volumus*	we are willing
2nd Plural	*vultis*	you are willing
3rd Plural	*volunt*	they are willing

Day 3, Exercise 1: True or False

vincere...to conquer	***True***	False
credere ....to believe	***True***	False
ducere...to rule	True	***False***
currere..to run	***True***	False
mittere...to eat	True	***False***
tempus, temporis (n)............................time	***True***	False
civis, civis (m/f)..................................state	True	***False***
dux, ducis (m).......................................leader	***True***	False
lex, legis...light	True	***False***
saepe..often	***True***	False

Day 3, Exercise 2: Match.

Future Tense Regular *(I will call)*   I call.

Future Tense Possible *(May I call)*   I will call.

Present Tense *(I call)*   I was calling.

Past Tense *(I was calling)*   May I call.

Day 3, Exercise 3: Rules.

The "ire" verbs love their ***i's***. They also copycat the -ere verbs.

In the present tense, for -ere verbs, you change the "e" of the stem to ***i***.

In the future tense regular, for -ere verbs, you ***leave the stem alone***.

In the future tense possible, for -ere verbs, you ***change the "e" to an "a"***.

In the past tense, for -ere verbs, you add ***ba*** to the stem, and then add the ending.

Day 3, Exercise 4: Fill in the blanks.

	Word	Meaning
1st Singular	*eram*	I was
2nd Singular	*eras*	you were
3rd Singular	*erat*	he was
1st Plural	*eramus*	we were
2nd Plural	*eratis*	you were
3rd Plural	*erant*	they were

	Word	Meaning
1st Singular	*possum*	I am able
2nd Singular	*potes*	you are able
3rd Singular	*potest*	he is able
1st Plural	*possumus*	we are able
2nd Plural	*potestis*	you are able
3rd Plural	*possunt*	they are able

	Word	Meaning
1st Singular	*ero*	I will be
2nd Singular	*eris*	you will be
3rd Singular	*erit*	it will be
1st Plural	*erimus*	we will be
2nd Plural	*eritis*	you will be
3rd Plural	*erunt*	they will be

	Word	Meaning
1st Singular	poteram	*I was able*
2nd Singular	poteras	*you were able*
3rd Singular	poterat	*he was able*
1st Plural	poteramus	*we were able*
2nd Plural	poteratis	*you were able*
3rd Plural	poterant	*they were able*

Day 4, Exercise 1: True or False

defendere.................................to conquer	True	***False***
scribere....................................to write	***True***	False
sentire......................................to rule	True	***False***
munire.....................................to build	***True***	False
dicere......................................to speak	***True***	False
rex, regis (m)..........................king	***True***	False
crux, crucis.............................cross	***True***	False
dolor, doloris..........................sorrow	***True***	False
panis, panis (m)......................peace	True	***False***
mons, montis (m)....................mountain	***True***	False
homo, hominis (m).................man	***True***	False
arbor, arboris (f.....................flower	True	***False***
sol, solis (m)...........................summit	True	***False***

Day 4, Exercise 2: Decline the following nouns by completing the chart.

Remember your neuter accusatives are like the nominatives!

Nominative	rex
Genitive	regis
Dative	***regi***
Accusative	***regem***
Ablative	***rege***

(This exercise is continued on the next page.)

Nominative	mare
Genitive	maris
Dative	*mari*
Accusative	*mare*
Ablative	mari

Nominative	flumen
Genitive	fluminis
Dative	*flumini*
Accusative	*flumen*
Ablative	*flumine*

Nominative	pastor
Genitive	pastoris
Dative	*pastori*
Accusative	*pastorem*
Ablative	*pastore*

Day 4, Exercise 3: True or False

trahere..................................to draw	***True***	False
gerere...................................to write	True	***False***
discere..................................to teach	True	***False***
cedere...................................to yield	***True***	False
petere...................................to seek	***True***	False
mare, maris (m)....................horse	True	***False***
pastor, pastoris.....................pasture	True	***False***
gens, gentis..........................tribe	***True***	False
libertas, libertatis..................love	True	***False***
caritas, caritatis....................liberty	True	***False***
fons, fontis (m)....................tribe	True	***False***

Day 4, Exercise 4: Give the meaning of the following indeclinables.

non	***not***	diu	***for a long time***
saepe	***often***	bene	***well***
in (ablative)	***in, on***	in (accusative)	***into, onto***
ad (accusative)	***to, towards***	trans (accusative)	***across***
per (accusative)	***through***	contra (accusative)	***against***
ante (accusative)	***before***	post (accusative)	***after***
a, ab (ablative)	***by***	cum (ablative)	***with***
e, ex (ablative)	***out of***	de (ablative)	***from, down from***

Lesson XVII

ಬಂಡ

Go over these every day for 10 minutes.

VERBS

laudare	to praise	monēre	to warn
audire	to hear	agere	to act, to do
bibere	to drink	edere	to eat
vivere	to live	ponere	to put, to place
regere	to rule	vincere	to conquer
credere	to believe	ducere	to lead
currere	to run	mittere	to send
defendere	to defend	scribere	to write
sentire	to feel	munire	to build
dicere	to say	petere	to seek
trahere	to draw	gerere	to conduct, wage
discere	to learn	cedere	to yield

NOUNS

dolor, doloris	pain, sorrow	panis, panis (m)	bread
mons, montis (m)	mountain	crux, crucis	cross
homo, hominis (m)	man	urbs, urbis	city
flumen, fluminis	river	civitas, civitatis	state
pax, pacis	peace	caput, capitis	head
Caesar, Caesaris	Caesar	Cicero, Ciceronis (m)	Cicero
canis, canis (m/f)	dog	veritas, veritatis	truth
virgo, virginis	virgin	arbor, arboris (f)	tree
sol, solis (m)	sun	rex, regis (m)	king
tempus, temporis (n)	time	civis, civis (m/f)	citizen
dux, ducis (m)	leader	lux, lucis	light
lex, legis	law	gens, gentis	tribe
fons, fontis (m)	fountain	tentatio, tentationis	temptation
caritas, caritatis	love	libertas, libertatis	freedom, liberty
pastor, pastoris	shepherd	mare, maris	sea

SPECIAL INDECLINABLE* WORDS:

non	not	diu	for a long time
saepe	often	bene	well
in (ablative)	in, on	in (accusative)	into, onto
ad (accusative)	to, towards	trans (accusative)	across
per (accusative)	through	contra (accusative)	against
ante (accusative)	before	post (accusative)	after
a, ab (ablative)	by	cum (ablative)	with
de (ablative)	from, down from	e, ex (ablative)	out of

Indeclinable means they never change. They never change even an ending.

-o, or -m	I	-mus	we
-s	you (sing)	-tis	you
-t	he, she or it	-nt	they

sum, es, est, sumus, estis, sunt (I am, you are, he is, we are, you are, they are)

eram, eras, erat, eramus, eratis, erant (I was, you were, he was, we were, you were, they were)*

ero, eris, erit, erimus, eritis, erunt (I will be, you will be, he will be, we will be, you will be, they will be)*

possum, potes, potest, possumus, potestis, possunt (I am able, you are able, he is able, we are able, you are able, they are able)

poteram, poteras, poterat, poteramus, poteratis, poterant (I was able, you were able, he was able, we were able, you were able, they were able)

potero, poteris, poterit, poterimus, poteritis, poterunt (I will be able, you will be able, he will be able, we will be able, you will be able, they will be able)

volo, vis, vult, volumus, vultis, volunt (I am willing, you are willing, he is willing, we are willing, you are willing, they are willing)

nolo, non vis, non vult, nolumus, non vultis, nolunt (I am not willing, you are not willing, he is not willing, we are not willing, you are not willing, they are not willing)

malo, mavis, mavult, malumus, mavultis, malunt (I prefer, you prefer, he prefers, we prefer, you prefer, they prefer) (Prefer means "to be more willing")

fero, fers, fert, ferimus, fertis, ferunt (I bear, you bear, he bears, we bear, you bear, they bear)

Remember your rules for gender:

> **Feminine nouns usually end in s-o-x**
>
> **Neuter nouns usually end in l-a-n-c-e-t**
>
> **Masculine nouns end in er-r-or**
> **Words that clearly denote a person of a particular gender are in that gender.**
> **(Ex: Cicero is masculine)**

Remember the Latin names for English cases and how to get them:

> **Nominative = Subject = First Form**
>
> **Genitive = Possessive ('s or the object of "of") = Second Form**
>
> **Dative = Indirect Object (object of "for") = Stem + i**
>
> **Accusative MASCULINE AND FEMININE = Direct Object or Object of some prepositions = Stem + em**
>
> **Accusative NEUTER = Direct Object or Object of some prepositions = Same as Nominative Singular**
>
> **Ablative = Object of some prepositions = Stem + e**

A noun is i - stem if it.....

Ends in -is or -es in the nominative first form and has the same number of syllables in the first and second form.

Ends in -s or -x in the nominative first form and has a stem that ends in two consonants.

Ends in -al, -ar, or -e in the nominative first form (neuter nouns).

Day 1, Exercise 1: Answer these.

List four vocabulary words from your noun list that are masculine.

All possible answers: dolor, doloris; mons, montis; homo, hominis; Caesar, Caesaris; canis, canis; sol, solis; panis, panis; Cicero, Ciceronis; arbor, arboris; rex, regis; dux, ducis; pastor, pastoris; fons, fontis.

List four vocabulary words from your noun list that are feminine.

All possible answers: pax, pacis; canis, canis; virgo, virginis; crux, crucis; urbs, urbis; civitas, civitatis; veritas, veritatis; lex, legis; caritas, caritatis; civis, civis; lux, lucis; gens, gentis; tentatio, tentationis; libertas, libertatis; arbor, arboris,

List four vocabulary words from your noun list that are neuter.

All possible answers: flumen, fluminis; caput, capitis; tempus, temporis; mare, maris.

Day 1, Exercise 2: Circle the nominative/subjects, box the genitive/possessives, underline the accusative/direct objects, and dash underline the datives/ indirect objects (objects of for). Put parentheses around prepositions and their objects and label the prepositions with a "p". Also, make sure to underline the objects of accusative prepositions.

Before doing this exercises let's go over this in more detail.

Look at your list of prepositions in the vocabulary section.

First, put "p" above the prepositions you find in the below sentences. (See my "p" above "through" and "by" in the example sentence.)

Next find the object of the prepositions. It's the next real word. Make sure you put the parentheses around the whole phrase. See below. I found the object of "through" which was "road". I put a set of parentheses around "through the road". I crossed out "the", of course. I did the same things for "by" the "house". ("House" is the object of "by".)

(This exercise is continued on the next page.)

Finally, look at the vocabulary list to see if those prepositions took the accusative or the ablative. In my example, I saw that "through" took an accusative object. I saw that "by" took an ablative object. So, I underlined the object of "through" but not the object of "by".

Did you notice that I underlined the object when it was accusative, but not ablative? Look at the word "road" below. Notice I underlined it with a single underline. I also use single underlines for accusative/direct objects.

I use single underlines for accusative/direct objects and accusative/objects of prepositions. I use a single underline for all accusatives.

Example: ~~The~~ man's (cat) ran (through ~~the~~ road)(by ~~the~~ house).

Here are your sentences:

1. ~~The~~ (man) sent ~~the~~ letter for John (to ~~the~~ post office.)

2. Sarah's (cat) ran (from ~~the~~ house) (through ~~the~~ grass) (to ~~the~~ tree.)

3. ~~The~~ (man) of ~~the~~ moon eats cheese.

4. (Charles) ran (by ~~the~~ river.)

5. (God) sent us Jesus.

Day 2, Exercise 3: Circle the correct form:

lex	**(nominative)**	dative
solem	**(accusative)**	ablative
rege	**(ablative)**	nominative
mari	nominative	**(dative)**
flumine	genitive	**(ablative)**
caritatis	accusative	**(genitive)**
tempus	**(nominative)**	genitive

Day 2, Exercise 4: Do a complete synopsis of the verb 'sentire'.

A verb that loves its i will keep it, but otherwise it copycats the -ere verbs. It doesn't have to change the "e" to "i" for the present, because it is already an "i." However, it adds the "e" for the past and future, so it can be just like the third conjugation -ere words, but it doesn't lose its "i." It loves its "i." The future possible changes the "e" of the regular to an "a."

	Present	Past	Future Regulars	Future Possibles
1st Singular	*sentio*	*sentiebam*	*sentiam*	*sentiam*
2nd Singular	*sentis*	*sentiebas*	*senties*	*sentias*
3rd Singular	*sentit*	*sentiebat*	*sentiet*	*sentiat*
1st Plural	*sentimus*	*sentiebamus*	*sentiemus*	*sentiamus*
2nd Plural	*sentitis*	*sentiebatis*	*sentietis*	*sentiatis*
3rd Plural	*sentiunt*	*sentiebant*	*sentient*	*sentiant*

> A noun is i - stem if it.....
>
> Ends in -is or -es in the nominative first form and has the same number of syllables in the first and second form.
>
> Ends in -s or -x in the nominative first form and has a stem that ends in two consonants.
>
> Ends in -al, -ar, or -e in the nominative first form (neuter nouns).

Day 3, Exercise 5: Answer these.

As you were told before, i-stem nouns have an "i" not an "e" in the neuter ablative singular. You have only one neuter i-stem noun in the vocabuary list. What is it?

<u>mare</u>

List four vocabulary words from you noun list that are i-stem.

<u>*All possible answers: **mons, montis; canis, canis; panis, panis; urbs, urbis; fons, fontis; civis, civis; gens, gentis.***</u>

Day 3, Exercise 6: Translate following these steps:

> Step 1: Please circle the subject, box the possessives and underline the <u>direct objects</u>. Use a dashed line under the indirect object. Cross out the words, "the," "a," or "an." Put parentheses (around prepositional phrases using accusatives or ablatives). Make sure you write "p" above the preposition and <u>underline</u> the object of the preposition once if it is accusative and do nothing if the object is ablative.
>
> Step 2: Write the Latin word you would use on Line A above the word. Remember that there is no Latin word for "of," "for," "the," "a," or "an".
>
> Step 3: Write the stem of the words (which need the stem form) on line B.
>
> Step 4: Add the correct endings to complete the translation on line C.
>
> *(This exercise is continued on the next page.)*

1.

A. ***Cicero, Ciceronis   credere   NA   dux, ducis   NA   NA   gens, gentis***

B.   ***crede***   ***duc***

May   (Cicero)   believe   ~~the~~   leader   of   ~~the~~ |tribe.|

C.   ***Cicero***   ***credat***   ***ducem***   ***gentis.***

2.

A. ***Caesar, Caesaris   discere   NA   veritas, veritatis   NA   NA   dux, ducis***

B.   ***disce***   ***veritat***   ***duc***

(Caesar)   was learning   ~~the~~   truth   for   the   leader.

C.   ***Caesar***   ***discebat***   ***veritatem***   ***duci.***

Lesson XVIII

Go over these every day for 10 minutes.

VERBS

laudare	to praise	monēre	to warn
audire	to hear	agere	to act, to do
bibere	to drink	edere	to eat
vivere	to live	ponere	to put, to place
regere	to rule	vincere	to conquer
credere	to believe	ducere	to lead
currere	to run	mittere	to send
defendere	to defend	scribere	to write
sentire	to feel	munire	to build
dicere	to say	petere	to seek
trahere	to draw	gerere	to conduct, wage
discere	to learn	cedere	to yield

NOUNS

dolor, doloris	pain, sorrow	panis, panis (m)	bread
mons, montis (m)	mountain	crux, crucis	cross
homo, hominis (m)	man	urbs, urbis	city
flumen, fluminis	river	civitas, civitatis	state
pax, pacis	peace	caput, capitis	head
Caesar, Caesaris	Caesar	Cicero, Ciceronis (m)	Cicero
canis, canis (m/f)	dog	veritas, veritatis	truth
virgo, virginis	virgin	arbor, arboris (f)	tree
sol, solis (m)	sun	rex, regis (m)	king
tempus, temporis (n)	time	civis, civis (m/f)	citizen
dux, ducis (m)	leader	lux, lucis	light
lex, legis	law	gens, gentis	tribe
fons, fontis (m)	fountain	tentatio, tentationis	temptation
caritas, caritatis	love	libertas, libertatis	freedom, liberty
pastor, pastoris	shepherd	mare, maris	sea

SPECIAL INDECLINABLE* WORDS:

non	not	diu	for a long time
saepe	often	bene	well
in (ablative)	in, on	in (accusative)	into, onto
ad (accusative)	to, towards	trans (accusative)	across
per (accusative)	through	contra (accusative)	against
ante (accusative)	before	post (accusative)	after
a, ab (ablative)	by	cum (ablative)	with
de (ablative)	from, down from	e, ex (ablative)	out of

* Indeclinable means they never change. They never change even an ending.

-o, or -m	I	-mus	we
-s	you (sing)	-tis	you
-t	he, she, or it	-nt	they

sum, es, est, sumus, estis, sunt *(I am, you are, he is, we are, you are, they are)*

eram, eras, erat, eramus, eratis, erant *(I was, you were, he was, we were, you were, they were)*

ero, eris, erit, erimus, eritis, erunt *(I will be, you will be, he will be, we will be, you will be, they will be)*

possum, potes, potest, possumus, potestis, possunt *(I am able, you are able, he is able, we are able, you are able, they are able)*

poteram, poteras, poterat, poteramus, poteratis, poterant *(I was able, you were able, he was able, we were able, you were able, they were able)*

potero, poteris, poterit, poterimus, poteritis, poterunt *(I will be able, you will be able, he will be able, we will be able, you will be able, they will be able)*

volo, vis, vult, volumus, vultis, volunt *(I am willing, you are willing, he is willing, we are willing, you are willing, they are willing)*

nolo, non vis, non vult, nolumus, non vultis, nolunt *(I am not willing, you are not willing, he is not willing, we are not willing, you are not willing, they are not willing)*

malo, mavis, mavult, malumus, mavultis, malunt *(I prefer, you prefer, he prefers, we prefer, you prefer, they prefer) (Prefer means "to be more willing")*

fero, fers, fert, ferimus, fertis, ferunt *(I bear, you bear, he bears, we bear, you bear, they bear)*

Remember your rules for gender:

> **Feminine nouns usually end in s-o-x**
>
> **Neuter nouns usually end in l-a-n-c-e-t**
>
> **Masculine nouns end in er-r-or**
>
> **Words that clearly denote a person of a particular gender are in that gender.**
> **(Ex: Cicero is masculine)**

Remember the Latin names for English cases and how to get them:

> **Nominative = Subject = First Form**
>
> **Genitive = Possessive ('s or the object of "of") = Second Form**
>
> **Dative = Indirect Object (object of "for") = Stem + i**
>
> **Accusative <u>MASCULINE AND FEMININE</u> = Direct Object or Object of some prepositions = Stem + em**
>
> **Accusative <u>NEUTER</u> = Direct Object or Object of some prepositions = Same as Nominative Singular**
>
> **Ablative = Object of some prepositions = Stem + e**

> **A noun is i - stem if it.....**
>
> **Ends in -is or -es in the nominative first form and has the same number of syllables in the first and second form.**
>
> **Ends in -s or -x in the nominative first form and has a stem that ends in two consonants.**
>
> **Ends in -al, -ar, or -e in the nominative first form (neuter nouns).**

So far all of our nouns in translations are singular. Now we want to make plural nouns. Making plurals is easy in English, right?

singular: man   plural: men   singular: tree   plural: trees

Day 1, Exercise 1: Let's make the following nouns plural in English

shepherd	**_shepherds_**	dog	**_dogs_**
sea	**_seas_**	city	**_cities_**
river	**_rivers_**	bread	**_breads_**
liberty	**_liberties_**	sun	**_suns_**

Mostly to make a plural we had to change the endings of these words, right? Well, we change endings in Latin too to make plurals. But Latin is a bit more complex because we have different endings already for different cases, right? Take the Latin word for law. For example the nominative/subject form is "lex" and the genitive/possessive form is "legis". So, each case will have a different plural ending. Here are the **plural endings:**

> Nominative <u>MASCULINE AND FEMININE</u> = Subject = Stem + ES
>
> Nominative <u>NEUTER</u> = Subject = Stem + A
>
> Genitive = Possessive ('s or the object of "of") = Stem + UM
>
> Dative = Indirect Object (object of "for") = Stem + IBUS
>
> Accusative = Direct Object or Object of some prepositions = same as Nominative Plural
>
> Ablative = Object of some prepositions = Stem + IBUS

Day 1, Exercise 2: Compare the two charts you have for cases now. You have your singular charge and your plural chart. Please label these two charts correctly. Which is the singular chart? Which is the plural chart?

Singular CHART

Nominative = Subject = First Form

Genitive = Possessive ('s or the object of "of") = Second Form

Dative = Indirect Object (object of "for") = Stem + i

Accusative <u>MASCULINE AND FEMININE</u> = Direct Object or Object of some prepositions = Stem + em

Accusative <u>NEUTER</u> = Direct Object or Object of some prepositions = Same as Nominative Singular

Ablative = Object of some prepositions = Stem + e

Plural CHART

Nominative <u>MASCULINE AND FEMININE</u> = Subject = Stem + ES

Nominative <u>NEUTER</u> = Subject = Stem + A

Genitive = Possessive ('s or the object of "of") = Stem + UM

Dative = Indirect Object (object of "for") = Stem + IBUS

Accusative = Direct Object or Object of some prepositions = Same as Nominative Plural

Ablative = Object of some prepositions = Stem + IBUS

Did you notice the top chart has different ending rules for neuter accusatives and for masculine/feminine accusatives. The bottom chart has different ending rules for neuter nominatives and for masculine/feminine nominatives. Make sure you have these charts memorized.

Day 2, Exercise 3: Build these plurals:

Example word: *arbor, arboris*

1. Write down the second form of the noun: <u>arboris</u>
2. Subtract the -is: <u>-is</u>
3. Give the stem: <u>arbor</u>
4. Add the Ablative Plural ending to the stem: <u>arbor + ibus</u>

A. Word: caput, capitis

1. Write down the second form of the noun: <u>*capitis*</u>
2. Subtract the -is: <u>*-is*</u>
3. Give the stem: <u>*capit*</u>
4. Add the Genitive Plural ending to the stem: <u>*capit + um*</u>

B. Word: sol, solis

1. Write down the second form of the noun: <u>*solis*</u>
2. Subtract the -is: <u>*-is*</u>
3. Give the stem: <u>*sol*</u>
4. Add the Dative Plural ending to the stem: <u>*sol + ibus*</u>

C. Word: mons, montis

1. Write down the second form of the noun: <u>*montis*</u>
2. Subtract the -is: <u>*-is*</u>
3. Give the stem: <u>*mont*</u>
4. Add the Nominative plural ending to the stem: <u>*mont + es*</u>

Bonus: What would the Accusative Plural be? <u>*montes*</u>

(This exercise is continued on the next page.)

D. Word: tempus, temporis

1. Write down the second form of the noun: *__temporis__*

2. Subtract the -is: *__-is__*

3. Give the stem: *__tempor__*

4. Add the Nominative plural ending to the stem: *__tempor + a__*

Bonus: What would the Accusative Plural be? *__tempora__*

Day 2, Exercise 4: Complete the chart.

Gender	Case	Singular	Plural
M/F	Nominative = Subject	1st Form	Stem + ES
N			Stem + A
All	Genitive = Possessive	*2nd Form*	*Stem + um*
All	Dative = Indirect Object	*Stem + i*	*Stem + ibus*
M/F	Accusative = Direct Object or Objects of some prepositions	Stem + EM	Same as Nom.
N		Same as Nom.	
All	Ablative = Objects of some prepositions	*Stem + e*	*Stem + ibus*

Day 3, Exercise 5: Do a complete synopsis of the verb "currere".

A verb that loves its i will keep it, but otherwise it copycats the -ere verbs. It doesn't have to change the "e" to "i" for the present, because it is already an "i." However, it adds the "e" for the past and future, so it can be just like the third conjugation -ere words, but it doesn't lose its "i." It loves its "i." The future possible changes the "e" of the regular to an "a."

(This exercise is continued on the next page.)

	Present	Past	Future Regulars	Future Possibles
1st Singular	curro	currebam	curram	curram
2nd Singular	curris	currebas	curres	curras
3rd Singular	currit	currebat	curret	currat
1st Plural	currimus	currebamus	curremus	curramus
2nd Plural	curritis	currebatis	curretis	curratis
3rd Plural	currunt	currebant	current	currant

Day 3, Exercise 6: Notice these mixed up sentences. The prepositions are in Latin, but their objects are in English. Put the objects into proper Latin. All the objects are plural! So use this chart.

> Nominative MASCULINE AND FEMININE = Subject = Stem + ES
>
> Nominative NEUTER = Subject = Stem + A
>
> Genitive = Possessive ('s or the object of "of") = Stem + UM
>
> Dative = Indirect Object (object of "for") = Stem + IBUS
>
> Accusative = Direct Object or Object of some prepositions = Same as Nominative
>
> Ablative = Object of some prepositions = Stem + IBUS

1. contra the laws   contra ***leges***
2. cum the shepherds   cum ***pastoribus***
3. ab the cities   ab ***urbibus***

Lesson XIX

Go over these every day for 10 minutes.

VERBS

laudare	to praise	monēre	to warn
audire	to hear	agere	to act, to do
bibere	to drink	edere	to eat
vivere	to live	ponere	to put, to place
regere	to rule	vincere	to conquer
credere	to believe	ducere	to lead
currere	to run	mittere	to send
defendere	to defend	scribere	to write
sentire	to feel	munire	to build
dicere	to say	petere	to seek
trahere	to draw	gerere	to conduct, wage
discere	to learn	cedere	to yield

NOUNS

dolor, doloris	pain, sorrow	panis, panis (m)	bread
mons, montis (m)	mountain	crux, crucis	cross
homo, hominis (m)	man	urbs, urbis	city
flumen, fluminis	river	civitas, civitatis	state
pax, pacis	peace	caput, capitis	head
Caesar, Caesaris	Caesar	Cicero, Ciceronis (m)	Cicero
canis, canis (m/f)	dog	veritas, veritatis	truth
virgo, virginis	virgin	arbor, arboris (f)	tree
sol, solis (m)	sun	rex, regis (m)	king
tempus, temporis (n)	time	civis, civis (m/f)	citizen
dux, ducis (m)	leader	lux, lucis	light
lex, legis	law	gens, gentis	tribe
fons, fontis (m)	fountain	tentatio, tentationis	temptation
caritas, caritatis	love	libertas, libertatis	freedom, liberty
pastor, pastoris	shepherd	mare, maris	sea

SPECIAL INDECLINABLE* WORDS:

non	not	diu	for a long time
saepe	often	bene	well
in (ablative)	in, on	in (accusative)	into, onto
ad (accusative)	to, towards	trans (accusative)	across
per (accusative)	through	contra (accusative)	against
ante (accusative)	before	post (accusative)	after
a, ab (ablative)	by	cum (ablative)	with
de (ablative)	from, down from	e, ex (ablative)	out of

* *Indeclinable means they never change. They never change even an ending.*

-o, or -m	I	-mus	we
-s	you (sing)	-tis	you
-t	he, she, or it	-nt	they

sum, es, est, sumus, estis, sunt *(I am, you are, he is, we are, you are, they are)*

eram, eras, erat, eramus, eratis, erant *(I was, you were, he was, we were, you were, they were)*

ero, eris, erit, erimus, eritis, erunt *(I will be, you will be, he will be, we will be, you will be, they will be)*

possum, potes, potest, possumus, potestis, possunt *(I am able, you are able, he is able, we are able, you are able, they are able)*

poteram, poteras, poterat, poteramus, poteratis, poterant *(I was able, you were able, he was able, we were able, you were able, they were able)*

potero, poteris, poterit, poterimus, poteritis, poterunt *(I will be able, you will be able, he will be able, we will be able, you will be able, they will be able)*

volo, vis, vult, volumus, vultis, volunt *(I am willing, you are willing, he is willing, we are willing, you are willing, they are willing)*

nolo, non vis, non vult, nolumus, non vultis, nolunt *(I am not willing, you are not willing, he is not willing, we are not willing, you are not willing, they are not willing)*

malo, mavis, mavult, malumus, mavultis, malunt *(I prefer, you prefer, he prefers, we prefer, you prefer, they prefer)* (Prefer means "to be more willing")

fero, fers, fert, ferimus, fertis, ferunt *(I bear, you bear, he bears, we bear, you bear, they bear)*

Remember your rules for gender:

> Feminine nouns usually end in s-o-x
>
> Neuter nouns usually end in l-a-n-c-e-t
>
> Masculine nouns end in er-r-or
>
> Words that clearly denote a person of a particular gender are in that gender.
> (Ex: Cicero is masculine)

Remember the Latin names for English cases and how to get them:

> **SINGULAR CHART**
>
> **Nominative** = Subject = First Form
>
> **Genitive** = Possessive ('s or the object of "of") = Second Form
>
> **Dative** = Indirect Object (object of "for") = Stem + i
>
> **Accusative MASCULINE AND FEMININE** = Direct Object or Object of some prepositions = Stem + em
>
> **Accusative NEUTER** = Direct Object or Object of some prepositions = Same as Nominative Singular
>
> **Ablative** = Object of some prepositions = Stem + e
>
>
> **PLURAL CHART**
>
> **Nominative MASCULINE AND FEMININE** = Subject = Stem + ES
>
> **Nominative NEUTER** = Subject = Stem + A
>
> **Genitive** = Possessive ('s or the object of "of") = Stem + UM
>
> **Dative** = Indirect Object (object of "for") = Stem + IBUS
>
> **Accusative** = Direct Object or Object of some prepositions = Same as Nominative Plural
>
> **Ablative** = Object of some prepositions = Stem + IBUS

i-Stem Rules

A noun is i - stem if it.....

Ends in -is or -es in the nominative first form and has the same number of syllables in the first and second form.

Ends in -s or -x in the nominative first form and has a stem that ends in two consonants.

Ends in -al, -ar, or -e in the nominative first form (neuter nouns).

Day 1, Exercise 1: Circle the nominative/subjects, box the genitive/possessives, underline the accusative/direct objects, and dash underline the datives/indirect objects (objects of for). Put parentheses around prepositions and their objects and label the prepositions with a "p". Also, make sure to underline the objects of accusative prepositions.

Before doing this exercises let's go over this in more detail.

Look at your list of prepositions in the vocabulary section.

First, put "p" above the prepositions you find in the below sentences. (See my "p" above "through" and "by" in the example sentence.)

Next find the object of the prepositions. It's the next real word. Make sure you put the parentheses around the whole phrase. See below. I found the object of "through" which was "road". I put a set of parentheses around "through the road". I crossed out "the", of course. I did the same things for "by" the "house". ("House" is the object of "by".)

Finally, look at the vocabulary list to see if those prepositions took the accusative or the ablative. In my example, I saw that "through" took an accusative object. I saw that "by" took an ablative object. So, I underlined the object of "through" but not the object of "by".

Did you notice that I underlined the object when it was accusative, but not ablative? Look at the word "road" below. Notice I underlined it with a single underline. I also use single underlines for accusative/direct objects.

I use single underlines for accusative/direct objects and accusative/objects of prepositions. I use a single underline for all accusatives.

Example: ~~The~~ |man's| (cat) ran (through ~~the~~ road)(by ~~the~~ house).
                                                      p   *p*

Here are your sentences:

1. ~~The~~ (man) ate cabbages (*p* in ~~the~~ garden.)

2. ~~The~~ (man) may be ~~a~~ rabbit (*p* in disguise.)

3. ~~The~~ (man) is not putting cabbages (*p* in ~~the~~ house) (*p* on ~~the~~ table.)

4. ~~The~~ (man) is putting cabbages (*p* in ~~a~~ hole) (*p* in ~~the~~ ground.)

5. ~~The~~ (man) is sharing ~~a~~ treat (*p* with ~~the~~ rabbits.)

Day 1, Exercise 2: Complete the chart.

Gender	Case	Singular	Plural
M/F	Nominative = Subject	1st form	Stem + es
N			Stem + a
All	Genitive = Possessive	2nd form	Stem + um
All	Dative = Indirect Object	Stem + i	Stem + ibus
M/F	Accusative = Direct Object or Objects of some prepositions	Stem + em	Same as nom
N		Same as nom	
All	Ablative = Objects of some prepositions	Stem + e	Stem + ibus

Day 2, Exercise 3: Circle the correct form:

Example:

lex	***nominative***	dative
soles	***accusative***	ablative
regibus	***ablative***	nominative
fluminum	nominative	***genitive***
caritates	genitive	***accusative***
hominis	accusative	***genitive***
tempora	***nominative***	genitive

Beginning Latin II - Lesson XIX

Day 2, Exercise 4: Give the plurals of each of the following words. Give the plural in the same case as the words are in. The first is done for you.

pastorem	*pastores*	lege	*legibus*
canem	*canes*	tempus	*tempora*
caput	*capita*	pani	*panibus*
lucem	*luces*	arbor	*arbores*

Day 3, Exercise 5: Fill in these charts.

A verb that loves its i will keep it, but otherwise it copycats the -ere verbs. It doesn't have to change the "e" to "i" for the present, because it is already an "i." However, it adds the "e" for the past and future, so it can be just like the third conjugation -ere words, but it doesn't lose its "i." It loves its "i." The future possible changes the "e" of the regular to an "a."

	Present	Past	Future Regulars	Future Possibles
2nd Singular	*audis*	audiebas	*audies*	*audias*

	Present	Past	Future Regulars	Future Possibles
3rd Singular	*trahit*	*trahebat*	trahet	*trahat*

	Present	Past	Future Regulars	Future Possibles
1st Plural	currimus	currebamus	curremus	curramus

Day 3, Exercise 6: Translate following these steps. Watch out for plurals. Remember, if the subject/nominative is a plural, then the verb must have a plural ending. If you have "the leader eats" then your verb is "edit" because "leader" is singular. But if you have "the leaders eat" then your verb is "edunt" because "leaders" is plural.

Step 1: Please circle the subject, box the possessives and underline the direct objects. Use a dashed line under the indirect object. Cross out the words, "the," "a," or "an." Put parentheses (around prepositional phrases using accusatives or ablatives). Make sure you write "p" above the preposition and underline the object of the preposition once if it is accusative and do nothing if the object is ablative.

Step 2: Write the Latin word you would use on Line A above the word. Remember that there is no Latin word for "of," "for," "the," "a," or "an".

Step 3: Write the stem of the words (which need the stem form) on line B.

Step 4: Add the correct endings to complete the translation on line C.

1.

A. *NA dux, ducis   mittere   panis, panis   NA   NA   gens, gentis*

B. *duc*   *mitte*   *pan*   *gent*

The (leaders)   send   bread   for   the   tribes.

C. *Duces*   *mittunt*   *panem*   *gentibus.*

Lesson XX

Go over these every day for 10 minutes.

VERBS

laudare	to praise	monēre	to warn
audire	to hear	agere	to act, to do
bibere	to drink	edere	to eat
vivere	to live	ponere	to put, to place
regere	to rule	vincere	to conquer
credere	to believe	ducere	to lead
currere	to run	mittere	to send
defendere	to defend	scribere	to write
sentire	to feel	munire	to build
dicere	to say	petere	to seek
trahere	to draw	gerere	to conduct, wage
discere	to learn	cedere	to yield

NOUNS

dolor, doloris	pain, sorrow	panis, panis (m)	bread
mons, montis (m)	mountain	crux, crucis	cross
homo, hominis (m)	man	urbs, urbis	city
flumen, fluminis	river	civitas, civitatis	state
pax, pacis	peace	caput, capitis	head
Caesar, Caesaris	Caesar	Cicero, Ciceronis (m)	Cicero
canis, canis (m/f)	dog	veritas, veritatis	truth
virgo, virginis	virgin	arbor, arboris (f)	tree
sol, solis (m)	sun	rex, regis (m)	king
tempus, temporis (n)	time	civis, civis (m/f)	citizen
dux, ducis (m)	leader	lux, lucis	light
lex, legis	law	gens, gentis	tribe
fons, fontis (m)	fountain	tentatio, tentationis	temptation
caritas, caritatis	love	libertas, libertatis	freedom, liberty
pastor, pastoris	shepherd	mare, maris	sea

SPECIAL INDECLINABLE* WORDS:

non	not	diu	for a long time
saepe	often	bene	well
in (ablative)	in, on	in (accusative)	into, onto
ad (accusative)	to, towards	trans (accusative)	across
per (accusative)	through	contra (accusative)	against
ante (accusative)	before	post (accusative)	after
a, ab (ablative)	by	cum (ablative)	with
de (ablative)	from, down from	e, ex (ablative)	out of

* Indeclinable means they never change. They never change even an ending.

-o, or -m	I	-mus	we
-s	you (sing)	-tis	you
-t	he, she, or it	-nt	they

sum, es, est, sumus, estis, sunt *(I am, you are, he is, we are, you are, they are)*

eram, eras, erat, eramus, eratis, erant *(I was, you were, he was, we were, you were, they were)*

ero, eris, erit, erimus, eritis, erunt *(I will be, you will be, he will be, we will be, you will be, they will be)*

possum, potes, potest, possumus, potestis, possunt *(I am able, you are able, he is able, we are able, you are able, they are able)*

poteram, poteras, poterat, poteramus, poteratis, poterant *(I was able, you were able, he was able, we were able, you were able, they were able)*

potero, poteris, poterit, poterimus, poteritis, poterunt *(I will be able, you will be able, he will be able, we will be able, you will be able, they will be able)*

volo, vis, vult, volumus, vultis, volunt *(I am willing, you are willing, he is willing, we are willing, you are willing, they are willing)*

nolo, non vis, non vult, nolumus, non vultis, nolunt *(I am not willing, you are not willing, he is not willing, we are not willing, you are not willing, they are not willing)*

malo, mavis, mavult, malumus, mavultis, malunt *(I prefer, you prefer, he prefers, we prefer, you prefer, they prefer) (Prefer means "to be more willing")*

fero, fers, fert, ferimus, fertis, ferunt *(I bear, you bear, he bears, we bear, you bear, they bear)*

Remember your rules for gender:

> **Feminine nouns usually end in s-o-x**
>
> **Neuter nouns usually end in l-a-n-c-e-t**
>
> **Masculine nouns end in er-r-or**
>
> **Words that clearly denote a person of a particular gender are in that gender.**
>
> **(Ex: Cicero is masculine)**

Remember the Latin names for English cases and how to get them:

> **SINGULAR CHART**
>
> **Nominative = Subject = First Form**
>
> **Genitive = Possessive ('s or the object of "of") = Second Form**
>
> **Dative = Indirect Object (object of "for") = Stem + i**
>
> **Accusative <u>MASCULINE AND FEMININE</u> = Direct Object or Object of some prepositions = Stem + em**
>
> **Accusative <u>NEUTER</u> = Direct Object or Object of some prepositions = Same as Nominative Singular**
>
> **Ablative = Object of some prepositions = Stem + e**
>
>
> **PLURAL CHART**
>
> **Nominative <u>MASCULINE AND FEMININE</u> = Subject = Stem + ES**
>
> **Nominative <u>NEUTER</u> = Subject = Stem + A**
>
> **Genitive = Possessive ('s or the object of "of") = Stem + UM**
>
> **Dative = Indirect Object (object of "for) = Stem + IBUS**
>
> **Accusative = Direct Object or Object of some prepositions = Same as Nominative Plural**
>
> **Ablative = Object of some prepositions = Stem +IBUS**

I-Stem Rules

> **A noun is i - stem if it.....**
>
> **Ends in -is or -es in the nominative first form and has the same number of syllables in the first and second form.**
>
> **Ends in -s or -x in the nominative first form and has a stem that ends in two consonants.**
>
> **Ends in -al, -ar, or -e in the nominative first form (neuter nouns).**

Day 1, Exercise 1: Circle the nominative/subjects, box the genitive/possessives, underline the accusative/direct objects, and dash underline the datives/indirect objects (objects of for). Put parentheses around prepositions and their objects and label the prepositions with a "p". Also, make sure to underline the objects of accusative prepositions.

Before doing this exercises let's go over this in more detail.

Look at your list of prepositions in the vocabulary section.

First, put "p" above the prepositions you find in the below sentences. (See my "p" above "through" and "by" in the example sentence.)

Next find the object of the prepositions. It's the next real word. Make sure you put the arentheses around the whole phrase. See below. I found the object of "through" which was "road". I put a set of parentheses around "through the road". I crossed out "the", of course. I did the same things for "by" the "house". ("House" is the object of "by".)

Finally, look at the vocabulary list to see if those prepositions took the accusative or the ablative. In my example, I saw that "through" took an accusative object. I saw that "by" took an ablative object. So, I underlined the object of "through" but not the object of "by".

Did you notice that I underlined the object when it was accusative, but not ablative? Look at the word "road" below. Notice I underlined it with a single underline. I also use single underlines for accusative/direct objects.

I use single underlines for accusative/direct objects and accusative/objects of prepositions. I use a single underline for all accusatives.

Example: ~~The~~ [man's] (cat) ran (through ~~the~~ road)(by ~~the~~ house).

Here are your sentences:

1. ~~The~~ (dog) barked (by ~~the~~ house.)

2. ~~The~~ (dog) was barking for ~~the~~ master.

3. ~~The~~ (master) heard ~~the~~ dog.

4. ~~The~~ (master) looks (in ~~the~~ [dog's] house.)

5. ~~A~~ (cat) was sleeping (in it.)

Day 1, Exercise 2: Fill in the blanks:

Word bank: sox, stem, lancet, consonants, error, neuter, syllables

Masculine nouns end in **_error_**. Feminine nouns end in **_sox_**. Neuter nouns end in **_lancet_**. Nouns are i-stem if they end in -is or -es in the Nominative/First Form and have the same number of **_syllables_** in the first two forms. Nouns are i-stem if they end in -s or - x in the Nominative/First Form and have a **_stem_** that ends in two **_consonants_**. **_Neuter_** i-stem nouns end in al-ar-e.

Day 2, Exercise 3: Complete the chart.

Gender	Case	Singular	Plural
M/F	Nominative = Subject	1st form	Stem + es
N			Stem + a
All	Genitive = Possessive	2nd form	Stem + um
All	Dative = Indirect Object	Stem + i	Stem + ibus
M/F	Accusative = Direct Object or Objects of some prepositions	Stem + em	Same as nom
N		Same as nom	
All	Ablative = Objects of some prepositions	Stem + e	Stem + ibus

Day 2, Exercise 4: Circle the correct form:

Example:

lex	**_nominative_**	dative
mari	accusative	**_dative_**
mari*	**_ablative_**	nominative
pastores	**_nominative_**	genitive
caritatis	**_genitive_**	accusative
hominibus	**_dative_**	genitive
capitis	nominative	**_genitive_**

*Remember the i-stems have an -i in the neuter ablative!

Day 3, Exercise 5: Fill in these charts. Use 'edere'.

A verb that loves its "i" will keep it, but otherwise it copycats the –ere verbs. It doesn't have to change the "e" to "i" for the present, because it is already an "i." However, it adds the "e" for the past and future, so it can be just like the third conjugation -ere words, but it doesn't lose its "i." It loves its "i."

	Present	Past	Future Regulars	Future Possibles
1st Singular	edo	edebam	edam	edam
2nd Singular	edis	edebas	edes	edas
3rd Singular	edit	edebat	edet	edat
1st Plural	edimus	edebamus	edemus	edamus
2nd Plural	editis	edebatis	edetis	edatis
3rd Plural	edunt	edebant	edent	edant

Day 3, Exercise 6: Translate following these steps:

Step 1: Please circle the subject, box the possessives and underline the <u>direct objects</u>. Use a dashed line under the indirect object. Cross out the words, "the," "a," or "an." Put parentheses (around prepositional phrases using accusatives or ablatives). Make sure you write "p" above the preposition and <u>underline</u> the object of the preposition once if it is accusative and do nothing if the object is ablative.

Step 2: Write the Latin word you would use on Line A above the word. Remember that there is no Latin word for "of," "for," "the," "a," or "an".

Step 3: Write the stem of the words (which need the stem form) on line B.

Step 4: Add the correct endings to complete the translation on line C.

1.

A. *NA*   *canis, canis*   *edere*   *NA*   *homo, hominis*   *panis, panis*

B.   *can*   *ede*   *homin*   *pan*

~~The~~   (dogs)   were eating   ~~the~~   [man's]   breads.

C.   *Canes*   *edebant*   *hominis*   *panes*.

Lesson XXI

Go over these every day for 10 minutes.

VERBS

laudare	to praise	monēre	to warn
audire	to hear	agere	to act, to do
bibere	to drink	edere	to eat
vivere	to live	ponere	to put, to place
regere	to rule	vincere	to conquer
credere	to believe	ducere	to lead
currere	to run	mittere	to send
defendere	to defend	scribere	to write
sentire	to feel	munire	to build
dicere	to say	petere	to seek
trahere	to draw	gerere	to conduct, wage
discere	to learn	cedere	to yield

NOUNS

dolor, doloris	pain, sorrow	panis, panis (m)	bread
mons, montis (m)	mountain	crux, crucis	cross
homo, hominis (m)	man	urbs, urbis	city
flumen, fluminis	river	civitas, civitatis	state
pax, pacis	peace	caput, capitis	head
Caesar, Caesaris	Caesar	Cicero, Ciceronis (m)	Cicero
canis, canis (m/f)	dog	veritas, veritatis	truth
virgo, virginis	virgin	arbor, arboris (f)	tree
sol, solis (m)	sun	rex, egis (m)	king
tempus, temporis (n)	time	civis, civis (m/f)	citizen
dux, ducis (m)	leader	lux, lucis	light
lex, legis	law	gens, gentis	tribe
fons, fontis (m)	fountain	tentatio, tentationis	temptation
caritas, caritatis	love	libertas, libertatis	freedom, liberty
pastor, pastoris	shepherd	mare, maris	sea

Beginning Latin II - Lesson XXI

SPECIAL INDECLINABLE* WORDS:

| non | not | diu | for a long time |
| saepe | often | bene | well |

in (ablative)	in, on	in (accusative)	into, onto
ad (accusative)	to, towards	trans (accusative)	across
per (accusative)	through	contra (accusative)	against
ante (accusative)	before	post (accusative)	after
a, ab (ablative)	by	cum (ablative)	with
de (ablative)	from, down from	e, ex (ablative)	out of

Indeclinable means they never change. They never change even an ending.

-o, or –m	I	-mus	we
-s	you (sing)	-tis	you
-t	he, she, or it	-nt	they

sum, es, est, sumus, estis, sunt *(I am, you are, he is, we are, you are, they are)*

eram, eras, erat, eramus, eratis, erant *(I was, you were, he was, we were, you were, they were)*

ero, eris, erit, erimus, eritis, erunt *(I will be, you will be, he will be, we will be, you will be, they will be)*

possum, potes, potest, possumus, potestis, possunt *(I am able, you are able, he is able, we are able, you are able, they are able)*

poteram, poteras, poterat, poteramus, poteratis, poterant *(I was able, you were able, he was able, we were able, you were able, they were able)*

potero, poteris, poterit, poterimus, poteritis, poterunt *(I will be able, you will be able, he will be able, we will be able, you will be able, they will be able)*

volo, vis, vult, volumus, vultis, volunt *(I am willing, you are willing, he is willing, we are willing, you are willing, they are willing)*

nolo, non vis, non vult, nolumus, non vultis, nolunt *(I am not willing, you are not willing, he is not willing, we are not willing, you are not willing, they are not willing)*

malo, mavis, mavult, malumus, mavultis, malunt *(I prefer, you prefer, he prefers, we prefer, you prefer, they prefer) (Prefer means "to be more willing")*

fero, fers, fert, ferimus, fertis, ferunt *(I bear, you bear, he bears, we bear, you bear, they bear)*

Remember your rules for gender:

> **Feminine nouns usually end in s-o-x**
>
> **Neuter nouns usually end in l-a-n-c-e-t**
>
> **Masculine nouns end in er-r-or**
>
> **Words that clearly denote a person of a particular gender are in that gender.
> (Ex: Cicero is masculine)**

Remember the Latin names for English cases and how to get them:

> **SINGULAR CHART**
>
> **Nominative = Subject = First Form**
>
> **Genitive = Possessive ('s or the object of "of") = Second Form**
>
> **Dative = Indirect Object (object of "for") = Stem + i**
>
> **Accusative MASCULINE AND FEMININE = Direct Object or Object of some prepositions = Stem + em**
>
> **Accusative NEUTER = Direct Object or Object of some prepositions = Same as Nominative**
>
> **Ablative = Object of some prepositions = Stem + e**
>
> **PLURAL CHART**
>
> **Nominative MASCULINE AND FEMININE = Subject = Stem + ES**
>
> **Nominative NEUTER = Subject = Stem + A**
>
> **Genitive = Possessive ('s or the object of "of") = Stem + UM**
>
> **Dative = Indirect Object (object of "for") = Stem + IBUS**
>
> **Accusative = Direct Object or Object of some prepositions = Same as Nominative**
>
> **Ablative = Object of some prepositions = Stem +IBUS**

i-Stem Rules

> **A noun is i-stem if it…..**
>
> Ends in -is or -es in the nominative first form and has the same number of syllables in the first and second form.
>
> Ends in -s or -x in the nominative first form and has a stem that ends in two consonants.
>
> Ends in -al, -ar, or -e in the nominative first form (neuter nouns).

❀ Beginning Latin II - Lesson XXI ❀

Day 1, Exercise 1: Matching

Nominative *(circle)*

Genitive *(box)*

Dative *(dash underline)*

Accusative *(underline)*

Day 1, Exercise 2: Complete the chart.

Gender	Case	Singular	Plural
M/F	Nominative = Subject	1st form	Stem + es
N			Stem + a
All	Genitive = Possessive	2nd form	Stem + um
All	Dative = Indirect Object	Stem + i	Stem + ibus
M/F	Accusative = Direct Object or Objects of some prepositions	Stem + em	Same as nom
N		Same as nom	
All	Ablative = Objects of some prepositions	Stem + e	Stem + ibus

Day 2, Exercise 3: Fill in the blanks:

1. What is the nominative, plural of canis, canis?   *canes*

2. What is the genitive, singular of pastor, pastoris?   *pastoris*

3. What is the dative, plural of lux, lucis?   *lucibus*

4. What is the ablative, singular of arbor, arboris?   *arbore*

Day 2, Exercise 4: Look at the charts on the following two pages. Find the differences between these two charts:*

Write the differences here:

<u>***In the first chart, ablative singular is divided into "ablative masculine and feminine" and "ablative neuter" but in the second chart, there is no division. Also, in the first chart, neuter nominative plural is "stem + ia" but in the second chart it is "stem + a". Lastly, in the first chart, genitive plural is "stem + ium" but in the second chart it is "stem + um."***</u>

SINGULAR CHART

Nominative = Subject = First Form

Genitive = Possessive ('s or the object of "of") = Second Form

Dative = Indirect Object (object of "for") = Stem + i

Accusative <u>MASCULINE AND FEMININE</u> = Direct Object or Object of some prepositions = Stem + em

Accusative <u>NEUTER</u> = Direct Object or Object of some prepositions = Same as Nominative

Ablative <u>MASCULINE AND FEMININE</u> = Object of some prepositions = Stem + e

Ablative <u>NEUTER</u> = Object of some prepositions = Stem + i

PLURAL CHART

Nominative <u>MASCULINE AND FEMININE</u> = Subject = Stem + ES

Nominative <u>NEUTER</u> = Subject = Stem + IA

Genitive = Possessive ('s or the object of "of") = Stem + IUM

Dative = Indirect Object (object of "for") = Stem + IBUS

Accusative = Direct Object or Object of some prepositions = Same as Nominative

Ablative = Object of some prepositions = Stem + IBUS

SINGULAR CHART

Nominative = Subject = First Form

Genitive = Possessive ('s or the object of "of") = Second Form

Dative = Indirect Object (object of "for") = Stem + i

Accusative MASCULINE AND FEMININE = Direct Object or Object of some prepositions = Stem + em

Accusative NEUTER = Direct Object or Object of some prepositions = Same as Nominative

Ablative = Object of some prepositions = Stem + e

PLURAL CHART

Nominative MASCULINE AND FEMININE = Subject = Stem + ES

Nominative NEUTER = Subject = Stem + A

Genitive = Possessive ('s or the object of "of") = Stem + UM

Dative = Indirect Object (object of "for") = Stem + IBUS

Accusative = Direct Object or Object of some prepositions = Same as Nominative

Ablative = Object of some prepositions = Stem + IBUS

*Hint: There are two small differences in the plural chart. There is a major addition in the singular chart.

Day 3, Exercise 5: Fill in these charts

> A verb that loves its i will keep it, but otherwise it copycats the -ere verbs. It doesn't have to change the "e" to "i" for the present, because it is already an "i." However, it adds the "e" for the past and future, so it can be just like the third conjugation -ere words, but it doesn't lose its "i." It loves its "i." The future possible changes the "e" of the regular to an "a."

	Present	Past	Future Regulars	Future Possibles
1st Plural	*edimus*	edebamus	*edemus*	*edamus*

	Present	Past	Future Regulars	Future Possibles
1st Singular	*scribo*	*scribebam*	*scribam*	*scribam*

	Present	Past	Future Regulars	Future Possibles
1st Singular	*mitto*	*mittebam*	*mittam*	*mittam*

Day 3, Exercise 6: Translate following these steps:

> Step 1: Please circle the subject, box the possessives and underline the <u>direct objects</u>. Use a dashed line under the indirect object. Cross out the words, "the," "a," or "an." Put parentheses (around prepositional phrases using accusatives or ablatives). Make sure you write "p" above the preposition and <u>underline</u> the object of the preposition once if it is accusative and do nothing if the object is ablative.
>
> Step 2: Write the Latin word you would use on Line A above the word. Remember that there is no Latin word for "of," "for," "the," "a," or "an".
>
> Step 3: Write the stem of the words (which need the stem form) on line B.
>
> Step 4: Add the correct endings to complete the translation on line C.

1.

A.	<u>NA</u>	<u>dux, ducis</u>	<u>mittere</u>	<u>homo, hominis</u>	<u>ab</u>	<u>NA</u>	<u>mons, montis</u>
B.		<u>duc</u>	<u>mitte</u>	<u>homin</u>	(Ablative)		<u>mont</u>
	~~The~~	(leader)	was sending	<u>men</u>	(by	~~the~~	mountains.)
C.		<u>Dux</u>	<u>mittebat</u>	<u>homines</u>	<u>ab</u>		<u>montibus</u>

Lesson XXII

Go over these every day for 10 minutes.

VERBS

laudare	to praise	monēre	to warn
audire	to hear	agere	to act, to do
bibere	to drink	edere	to eat
vivere	to live	ponere	to put, to place
regere	to rule	vincere	to conquer
credere	to believe	ducere	to lead
currere	to run	mittere	to send
defendere	to defend	scribere	to write
sentire	to feel	munire	to build
dicere	to say	petere	to seek
trahere	to draw	gerere	to conduct, wage
discere	to learn	cedere	to yield

NOUNS

dolor, doloris	pain, sorrow	panis, panis (m)	bread
mons, montis (m)	mountain	crux, crucis	cross
homo, hominis (m)	man	urbs, urbis	city
flumen, fluminis	river	civitas, civitatis	state
pax, pacis	peace	caput, capitis	head
Caesar, Caesaris	Caesar	Cicero, Ciceronis (m)	Cicero
canis, canis (m/f)	dog	veritas, veritatis	truth
virgo, virginis	virgin	arbor, arboris (f)	tree
sol, solis (m)	sun	rex, egis (m)	king
tempus, temporis (n)	time	civis, civis (m/f)	citizen
dux, ducis (m)	leader	lux, lucis	light
lex, legis	law	gens, gentis	tribe
fons, fontis (m)	fountain	tentatio, tentationis	temptation
caritas, caritatis	love	libertas, libertatis	freedom, liberty
pastor, pastoris	shepherd	mare, maris	sea

SPECIAL INDECLINABLE* WORDS:

non	not	diu	for a long time
saepe	often	bene	well
in (ablative)	in, on	in (accusative)	into, onto
ad (accusative)	to, towards	trans (accusative)	across
per (accusative)	through	contra (accusative)	against
ante (accusative)	before	post (accusative)	after
a, ab (ablative)	by	cum (ablative)	with
de (ablative)	from, down from	e, ex (ablative)	out of

Indeclinable means they never change. They never change even an ending.

-o, or –m	I	-mus	we
-s	you (sing)	-tis	you
-t	he, she, or it	-nt	they

sum, es, est, sumus, estis, sunt *(I am, you are, he is, we are, you are, they are)*

eram, eras, erat, eramus, eratis, erant *(I was, you were, he was, we were, you were, they were)*

ero, eris, erit, erimus, eritis, erunt *(I will be, you will be, he will be, we will be, you will be, they will be)*

possum, potes, potest, possumus, potestis, possunt *(I am able, you are able, he is able, we are able, you are able, they are able)*

poteram, poteras, poterat, poteramus, poteratis, poterant *(I was able, you were able, he was able, we were able, you were able, they were able)*

potero, poteris, poterit, poterimus, poteritis, poterunt *(I will be able, you will be able, he will be able, we will be able, you will be able, they will be able)*

volo, vis, vult, volumus, vultis, volunt *(I am willing, you are willing, he is willing, we are willing, you are willing, they are willing)*

nolo, non vis, non vult, nolumus, non vultis, nolunt *(I am not willing, you are not willing, he is not willing, we are not willing, you are not willing, they are not willing)*

malo, mavis, mavult, malumus, mavultis, malunt *(I prefer, you prefer, he prefers, we prefer, you prefer, they prefer) (Prefer means "to be more willing")*

fero, fers, fert, ferimus, fertis, ferunt *(I bear, you bear, he bears, we bear, you bear, they bear)*

Remember your rules for gender:

> **Feminine nouns usually end in s-o-x**
>
> **Neuter nouns usually end in l-a-n-c-e-t**
>
> **Masculine nouns end in er-r-or**
>
> **Words that clearly denote a person of a particular gender are in that gender.**
>
> **(Ex: Cicero is masculine)**

Remember the Latin names for English cases and how to get them:

> **SINGULAR CHART**
>
> **Nominative = Subject = First Form**
>
> **Genitive = Possessive ('s or the object of "of") = Second Form**
>
> **Dative = Indirect Object (object of "for") = Stem + i**
>
> **Accusative MASCULINE AND FEMININE = Direct Object or Object of some prepositions = Stem + em**
>
> **Accusative NEUTER = Direct Object or Object of some prepositions = Same as Nominative**
>
> **Ablative = Object of some prepositions = Stem + e**
>
> **PLURAL CHART**
>
> **Nominative MASCULINE AND FEMININE = Subject = Stem + ES**
>
> **Nominative NEUTER = Subject = Stem + A**
>
> **Genitive = Possessive ('s or the object of "of") = Stem + UM**
>
> **Dative = Indirect Object (object of "for") = Stem + IBUS**
>
> **Accusative = Direct Object or Object of some prepositions = Same as Nominative**
>
> **Ablative = Object of some prepositions = Stem +IBUS**

i-Stem Rules

> **A noun is i-stem if it…..**
>
> **Ends in -is or -es in the nominative first form and has the same number of syllables in the first and second form.**
>
> **Ends in -s or -x in the nominative first form and has a stem that ends in two consonants.**
>
> **Ends in -al, -ar, or -e in the nominative first form (neuter nouns).**

Beginning Latin II - Lesson XXII

Day 1, Exercise 1: Matching

o _I_   you (plural)

s _you (singular)_   you (singular)

t _he, she, it_   I

mus _we_   we

tis _you (plural)_   he, she, it

nt _they_   they

Day 1, Exercise 2: Complete the chart.

Gender	Case	Singular	Plural
M/F	Nominative = Subject	*1ˢᵗ form*	*Stem + es*
N			*Stem + a*
All	Genitive = Possessive	*2ⁿᵈ form*	*Stem + um*
All	Dative = Indirect Object	*Stem + i*	*Stem + ibus*
M/F	Accusative = Direct Object or Objects of some prepositions	*Stem + em*	*Same as nom*
N		*Same as nom*	
All	Ablative = Objects of some prepositions	*Stem + e*	*Stem + ibus*

You know that there are differences in some cases between the masculine/feminine noun forms and the neuter noun forms. For example, singular accusative neuter endings are the same as the nominative ending, and singular accusative masculine/feminine ending is "stem + em". To help us know what gender a word is, we have certain rules: "error, sox and lancet". We also know i-stem rules and these rules give us a few more endings. You compared two charts last week. These two charts compared regular nouns to i stem nouns. You were asked to find the differences. You can see them in the chart below. The i-stem differences are underlined. You will note three differences in neuter i-stems compared to neuter regulars: ablative singular, nominative plural, and genitive plural. You will note one difference between masculine/feminine i-stem and masculine/feminine regular: genitive plural.

(INCLUDES I-STEMS)

SINGULAR CHART

Nominative = Subject = First Form

Genitive = Possessive ('s or the object of "of") = Second Form

Dative = Indirect Object (object of "for") = Stem + i

Accusative <u>MASCULINE AND FEMININE</u> = Direct Object or Object of some prepositions = Stem + em

Accusative <u>NEUTER</u> = Direct Object or Object of some prepositions = Same as Nominative Singular

Ablative = Object of some prepositions = Stem + e (Stem + i if NEUTER i-stem)

PLURAL CHART

Nominative <u>MASCULINE AND FEMININE</u> = Subject = Stem + ES

Nominative <u>NEUTER</u> = Subject = Stem + A (Stem + IA if i-stem)

Genitive = Possessive ('s or the object of "of") = Stem + UM <u>(Stem + ium if i-stem)</u>

Dative = Indirect Object (object of "for") = Stem + IBUS

Accusative = Direct Object or Object of some prepositions = Same as Nominative Plural

Ablative = Object of some prepositions = Stem + IBUS

Day 2, Exercise 3: Complete the chart for an i-stem word.

Gender	Case	Singular	Plural
M/F	Nominative = Subject	1st form	Stem + es
N			Stem + ia
All	Genitive = Possessive	2nd form	Stem + ium
All	Dative = Indirect Object	Stem + i	Stem + ibus
M/F	Accusative = Direct Object or Objects of some prepositions	Stem + em	Same as nom
N		Same as nom	
M/F	Ablative = Objects of some prepositions	Stem + e	Stem + ibus
N		Stem + i	

Day 2, Exercise 4:

The word "mare, maris" is i-stem, neuter. Fill in the following chart.

Which rule tells you "mare, maris" is neuter? **L-A-N-C-E-T**

Which rule tells you "mare, maris" is i-stem? **It is neuter and ends in "e"**

Nominative Singular:	mare	Nominative Plural:	mar*ia*
Genitive Singular:	maris	Genitive Plural:	mar*ium*
Dative Singular:	mar*i*	Dative Plural:	mar*ibus*
Accusative Singular:	mar*e*	Accusative Plural:	mar*ia*
Ablative Singular:	mar*i*	Ablative Plural:	mar*ibus*

(This exercise is continued on the next page.)

The word "urbs, urbis" is i-stem, feminine. Fill in the following chart. Which rule tells you that "urbs, urbis" is feminine? **_S-O-X_**

Which rule tells you that "urbs, urbis" is i-stem? **_It ends in "s" and has a stem that ends in two consonants._**

Nominative Singular:	urbs	Nominative Plural:	urb**_es_**
Genitive Singular:	urbis	Genitive Plural:	urb**_ium_**
Dative Singular:	urb**_i_**	Dative Plural:	urb**_ibus_**
Accusative Singular:	urb**_em_**	Accusative Plural:	urb**_es_**
Ablative Singular:	urb**_e_**		urb**_ibus_**

Day 3, Exercise 1: Do a complete synopsis of the verb 'discere.'

A verb that loves its "i" will keep it, but otherwise it copycats the -ere verbs. It doesn't have to change the "e" to "i" for the present, because it is already an "i." However, it adds the "e" for the past and future, so it can be just like the third conjugation -ere words, but it doesn't lose its "i." It loves its "i."

	Present	Past	Future Regulars	Future Possibles
1st Singular	disco	discebam	discam	discam
2nd Singular	discis	discebas	disces	discas
3rd Singular	discit	discebat	discet	discat
1st Plural	discimus	discebamus	discemus	discamus
2nd Plural	discitis	discebatis	discetis	discatis
3rd Plural	discunt	discebant	discent	discant

Day 3, Exercise 2: Translate following these steps:

Step 1: Please circle the subject, box the possessives and underline the direct objects. Use a dashed line under the indirect object. Cross out the words, "the," "a," or "an." Put parentheses (around prepositional phrases using accusatives or ablatives). Make sure you write "p" above the preposition and underline the object of the preposition once if it is accusative and do nothing if the object is ablative.

Step 2: Write the Latin word you would use on Line A above the word. Remember that there is no Latin word for "of," "for," "the," "a," or "an".

Step 3: Write the stem of the words (which need the stem form) on line B.

Step 4: Add the correct endings to complete the translation on line C.

1.

A. *NA*   *lex, legis*   *ducere*   *ad*   *NA*   *lux, lucis*   *in*   *tempus, temporis*

B.   *duc*   (Accusative)   *luc*   (Ablative)   *tempor*

~~The~~   (law)   will lead   (to   ~~the~~   light)   (in   time.)

C.   *Lex*   *ducet*   *ad*   *lucem*   *in*   *tempore.*

Lesson XXIII

Go over these every day for 10 minutes.

VERBS

laudare	to praise	monēre	to warn
audire	to hear	agere	to act, to do
bibere	to drink	edere	to eat
vivere	to live	ponere	to put, to place
regere	to rule	vincere	to conquer
credere	to believe	ducere	to lead
currere	to run	mittere	to send
defendere	to defend	scribere	to write
sentire	to feel	munire	to build
dicere	to say	petere	to seek
trahere	to draw	gerere	to conduct, wage
discere	to learn	cedere	to yield

NOUNS

dolor, doloris	pain, sorrow	panis, panis (m)	bread
mons, montis (m)	mountain	crux, crucis	cross
homo, hominis (m)	man	urbs, urbis	city
flumen, fluminis	river	civitas, civitatis	state
pax, pacis	peace	caput, capitis	head
Caesar, Caesaris	Caesar	Cicero, Ciceronis (m)	Cicero
canis, canis (m/f)	dog	veritas, veritatis	truth
virgo, virginis	virgin	arbor, arboris (f)	tree
sol, solis (m)	sun	rex, egis (m)	king
tempus, temporis (n)	time	civis, civis (m/f)	citizen
dux, ducis (m)	leader	lux, lucis	light
lex, legis	law	gens, gentis	tribe
fons, fontis (m)	fountain	tentatio, tentationis	temptation
caritas, caritatis	love	libertas, libertatis	freedom, liberty
pastor, pastoris	shepherd	mare, maris	sea

SPECIAL INDECLINABLE* WORDS:

non	not	diu	for a long time
saepe	often	bene	well
in (ablative)	in, on	in (accusative)	into, onto
ad (accusative)	to, towards	trans (accusative)	across
per (accusative)	through	contra (accusative)	against
ante (accusative)	before	post (accusative)	after
a, ab (ablative)	by	cum (ablative)	with
de (ablative)	from, down from	e, ex (ablative)	out of

* *Indeclinable means they never change. They never change even an ending.*

-o, or –m	I	-mus	we
-s	you (sing)	-tis	you
-t	he, she, or it	-nt	they

sum, es, est, sumus, estis, sunt *(I am, you are, he is, we are, you are, they are)*

eram, eras, erat, eramus, eratis, erant *(I was, you were, he was, we were, you were, they were)*

ero, eris, erit, erimus, eritis, erunt *(I will be, you will be, he will be, we will be, you will be, they will be)*

possum, potes, potest, possumus, potestis, possunt *(I am able, you are able, he is able, we are able, you are able, they are able)*

poteram, poteras, poterat, poteramus, poteratis, poterant *(I was able, you were able, he was able, we were able, you were able, they were able)*

potero, poteris, poterit, poterimus, poteritis, poterunt *(I will be able, you will be able, he will be able, we will be able, you will be able, they will be able)*

volo, vis, vult, volumus, vultis, volunt *(I am willing, you are willing, he is willing, we are willing, you are willing, they are willing)*

nolo, non vis, non vult, nolumus, non vultis, nolunt *(I am not willing, you are not willing, he is not willing, we are not willing, you are not willing, they are not willing)*

malo, mavis, mavult, malumus, mavultis, malunt *(I prefer, you prefer, he prefers, we prefer, you prefer, they prefer) (Prefer means "to be more willing")*

fero, fers, fert, ferimus, fertis, ferunt *(I bear, you bear, he bears, we bear, you bear, they bear)*

Remember your rules for gender:

Feminine nouns usually end in s-o-x

Neuter nouns usually end in l-a-n-c-e-t

Masculine nouns end in er-r-or

Words that clearly denote a person of a particular gender are in that gender.

(Ex: Cicero is masculine)

i-Stem Rules

A noun is i-stem if it…..

Ends in -is or -es in the nominative first form and has the same number of syllables in the first and second form.

Ends in -s or -x in the nominative first form and has a stem that ends in two consonants.

Ends in -al, -ar, or -e in the nominative first form (neuter nouns).

Noun Declensions

(INCLUDES I-STEMS)

SINGULAR CHART

Nominative = Subject = First Form

Genitive = Possessive ('s or the object of "of") = Second Form

Dative = Indirect Object (object of "for") = Stem + i

Accusative MASCULINE AND FEMININE = Direct Object or Object of some prepositions = Stem + em

Accusative NEUTER = Direct Object or Object of some prepositions = Same as Nominative Singular

Ablative = Object of some prepositions = Stem + e (Stem + i if NEUTER i-stem)

PLURAL CHART

Nominative MASCULINE AND FEMININE = Subject = Stem + ES

Nominative NEUTER = Subject = Stem + A (Stem +IA if i-stem)

Genitive = Possessive ('s or the object of "of") = Stem + UM (Stem + ium if i-stem)

Dative = Indirect Object (object of "for") = Stem + IBUS

Accusative = Direct Object or Object of some prepositions = Same as Nominative Plural

Ablative = Object of some prepositions = Stem + IBUS

Day 1, Exercise 1: Matching

error *(masculine)*   masculine
sox   *(feminine)*   neuter
lancet *(neuter)*   feminine

Day 1, Exercise 2: Complete the chart.

Gender	Case	Singular	Plural
M/F	Nominative = Subject	*1st form*	*Stem + es*
N			*Stem + a*
All	Genitive = Possessive	*2nd form*	*Stem + um*
All	Dative = Indirect Object	*Stem + i*	*Stem + ibus*
M/F	Accusative = Direct Object or Objects of some prepositions	*Stem + em*	*Same as nom*
N		*Same as nom*	
All	Ablative = Objects of some prepositions	*Stem + e*	*Stem + ibus*

Complete the chart for an i-stem word.

Gender	Case	Singular	Plural
M/F	Nominative = Subject	*1st form*	*Stem + es*
N			*Stem + ia*
All	Genitive = Possessive	*2nd form*	*Stem + ium*
All	Dative = Indirect Object	*Stem + i*	*Stem + ibus*
M/F	Accusative = Direct Object or Objects of some prepositions	*Stem + em*	*Same as nom*
N		*Same as nom*	
M/F	Ablative = Objects of some prepositions	*Stem + e*	*Stem + ibus*
N		*Stem + i*	

Day 2, Exercise 3: Fill in the following chart(s):

Which rule tells you "civis, civis" is masculine/feminine? ***It is an exception.***

Which rule tells you "civis, civis" is i-stem? ***Nominative ends in "is" and it has two syllables in each form.***

Nominative Singular:	civis	Nominative Plural:	civ***es***
Genitive Singular:	civis	Genitive Plural:	civ***ium***
Dative Singular:	civ***i***	Dative Plural:	civ***ibus***
Accusative Singular	civ***em***	Accusative Plural:	civ***es***
Ablative Singular	civ***e***	Ablative Plural:	civ***ibus***

Which rule tells you "lex, legis" is feminine? ***S-O-X.***

Which rule tells you "fons, fontis" is i-stem? ***Nominative ends in s and it has a stem ending in two consonants.***

Nominative Singular:	fons	Nominative Plural:	font***es***
Genitive Singular:	fontis	Genitive Plural:	font***ium***
Dative Singular:	font***i***	Dative Plural:	font***ibus***
Accusative Singular	font***em***	Accusative Plural:	font***es***
Ablative Singular	font***e***	Ablative Plural:	font***ibus***

Day 2, Exercise 4: Circle the correct form:

lex	***nominative***	dative
tempora	***accusative***	ablative
fontium	ablative	***genitive***
fluminum	nominative	***genitive***
montibus	***ablative***	accusative
lux	accusative	***nominative***
mari	***ablative***	genitive

Day 3, Exercise 5: Fill in these charts.

> A verb that loves its i will keep it, but otherwise it copycats the -ere verbs. It doesn't have to change the "e" to "i" for the present, because it is already an "i". However, it adds the "e" for the past and future, so it can be just like the third conjugation -ere words, but it doesn't lose its "i." It loves its "i." The future possible changes the "e" of the regular to an "a."

	Present	Past	Future Regulars	Future Possibles
2nd Plural	*editis*	*edebatis*	*edetis*	*edatis*

	Present	Past	Future Regulars	Future Possibles
3rd Plural	*audiunt*	*audiebant*	*audient*	*audiant*

	Present	Past	Future Regulars	Future Possibles
3rd Singular	*mittit*	*mittebat*	*mittet*	*mittat*

Day 3, Exercise 6: Translate following these steps:

Step 1: Please circle the subject, box the possessives and underline the direct objects. Use a dashed line under the indirect object. Cross out the words, "the," "a," or "an." Put parentheses (around prepositional phrases using accusatives or ablatives). Make sure you write "p" above the preposition and underline the object of the preposition once if it is accusative and do nothing if the object is ablative.

Step 2: Write the Latin word you would use on Line A above the word. Remember that there is no Latin word for "of," "for," "the," "a," or "an".

Step 3: Write the stem of the words (which need the stem form) on line B.

Step 4: Add the correct endings to complete the translation on line C.

1.

A. *NA pastor, pastoris*   *mittere*   *NA*   *NA*   *dux, ducis*   *NA*   *NA*   *gens, gentis*

B. *pastor*   *mitte*   *duc*   *gent*

~~The~~ (shepherds)   may send   for   the   leaders   of   the   tribes.

C. *Pastores*   *mittant*   *ducibus*   *gentium.*

210

Lesson XXIV

Go over these every day for 10 minutes.

VERBS

laudare	to praise	monēre	to warn
audire	to hear	agere	to act, to do
bibere	to drink	edere	to eat
vivere	to live	ponere	to put, to place
regere	to rule	vincere	to conquer
credere	to believe	ducere	to lead
currere	to run	mittere	to send
defendere	to defend	scribere	to write
sentire	to feel	munire	to build
dicere	to say	petere	to seek
trahere	to draw	gerere	to conduct, wage
discere	to learn	cedere	to yield

NOUNS

dolor, doloris	pain, sorrow	panis, panis (m)	bread
mons, montis (m)	mountain	crux, crucis	cross
homo, hominis (m)	man	urbs, urbis	city
flumen, fluminis	river	civitas, civitatis	state
pax, pacis	peace	caput, capitis	head
Caesar, Caesaris	Caesar	Cicero, Ciceronis (m)	Cicero
canis, canis (m/f)	dog	veritas, veritatis	truth
virgo, virginis	virgin	arbor, arboris (f)	tree
sol, solis (m)	sun	rex, egis (m)	king
tempus, temporis (n)	time	civis, civis (m/f)	citizen
dux, ducis (m)	leader	lux, lucis	light
lex, legis	law	gens, gentis	tribe
fons, fontis (m)	fountain	tentatio, tentationis	temptation
caritas, caritatis	love	libertas, libertatis	freedom, liberty
pastor, pastoris	shepherd	mare, maris	sea

Beginning Latin II - Lesson XXIV

SPECIAL INDECLINABLE* WORDS:

non	not	diu	for a long time
saepe	often	bene	well
in (ablative)	in, on	in (accusative)	into, onto
ad (accusative)	to, towards	trans (accusative)	across
per (accusative)	through	contra (accusative)	against
ante (accusative)	before	post (accusative)	after
a, ab (ablative)	by	cum (ablative)	with
de (ablative)	from, down from	e, ex (ablative)	out of

Indeclinable means they never change. They never change even an ending.

-o, or –m	I	-mus	we
-s	you (sing)	-tis	you
-t	he, she, or it	-nt	they

sum, es, est, sumus, estis, sunt *(I am, you are, he is, we are, you are, they are)*

eram, eras, erat, eramus, eratis, erant *(I was, you were, he was, we were, you were, they were)*

ero, eris, erit, erimus, eritis, erunt *(I will be, you will be, he will be, we will be, you will be, they will be)*

possum, potes, potest, possumus, potestis, possunt *(I am able, you are able, he is able, we are able, you are able, they are able)*

poteram, poteras, poterat, poteramus, poteratis, poterant *(I was able, you were able, he was able, we were able, you were able, they were able)*

potero, poteris, poterit, poterimus, poteritis, poterunt *(I will be able, you will be able, he will be able, we will be able, you will be able, they will be able)*

volo, vis, vult, volumus, vultis, volunt *(I am willing, you are willing, he is willing, we are willing, you are willing, they are willing)*

nolo, non vis, non vult, nolumus, non vultis, nolunt *(I am not willing, you are not willing, he is not willing, we are not willing, you are not willing, they are not willing)*

malo, mavis, mavult, malumus, mavultis, malunt *(I prefer, you prefer, he prefers, we prefer, you prefer, they prefer) (Prefer means "to be more willing")*

fero, fers, fert, ferimus, fertis, ferunt *(I bear, you bear, he bears, we bear, you bear, they bear)*

Gender Rules

Feminine nouns usually end in s-o-x

Neuter nouns usually end in l-a-n-c-e-t

Masculine nouns end in er-r-or

Words that clearly denote a person of a particular gender are in that gender.
(Ex: Cicero is masculine)

i-Stem Rules

A noun is i-stem if it….

Ends in -is or -es in the nominative first form and has the same number of syllables in the first and second form.

Ends in -s or -x in the nominative first form and has a stem that ends in two consonants.

Ends in -al, -ar, or -e in the nominative first form (neuter nouns).

Noun Declensions

(INCLUDES I-STEMS)

SINGULAR CHART

Nominative = Subject = First Form

Genitive = Possessive ('s or the object of "of") = Second Form

Dative = Indirect Object (object of "for") = Stem + i

Accusative <u>MASCULINE AND FEMININE</u> = Direct Object or Object of some prepositions = Stem + em

Accusative <u>NEUTER</u> = Direct Object or Object of some prepositions = Same as Nominative Singular

Ablative = Object of some prepositions = Stem + e (Stem + i if NEUTER i-stem)

PLURAL CHART

Nominative <u>MASCULINE AND FEMININE</u> = Subject = Stem + ES

Nominative <u>NEUTER</u> = Subject = Stem + A (Stem + IA if i-stem)

Genitive = Possessive ('s or the object of "of") = Stem + UM (<u>Stem + ium if i-stem</u>)

Dative = Indirect Object (object of "for") = Stem + IBUS

Accusative = Direct Object or Object of some prepositions = Same as Nominative Plural

Ablative = Object of some prepositions = Stem + IBUS

Day 1, Exercise 1: Matching

o *(I)*   you (plural)

s *(you, singular)*   we

t *(he, she, it)*   I

mus *(we)*   you (singular)

tis *(you, plural)*   he, she, it

nt *(they)*   they

Day 1, Exercise 2: Complete the chart.

Gender	Case	Singular	Plural
M/F	Nominative = Subject	*1st form*	*Stem + es*
N			*Stem + a*
All	Genitive = Possessive	*2nd form*	*Stem + um*
All	Dative = Indirect Object	*Stem + i*	*Stem + ibus*
M/F	Accusative = Direct Object or Objects of some prepositions	*Stem + em*	*Same as nom*
N		*Same as nom*	*Same as nom*
All	Ablative = Objects of some prepositions	*Stem + e*	*Stem + ibus*

(This exercise is continued on the next page.)

∞ Beginning Latin II - Lesson XXIV ∞

Complete the chart for an i-stem word.

Gender	Case	Singular	Plural
M/F	Nominative = Subject	1ˢᵗ form	*Stem + es*
N			*Stem + ia*
All	Genitive = Possessive	2ⁿᵈ form	*Stem + ium*
All	Dative = Indirect Object	*Stem + i*	*Stem + ibus*
M/F	Accusative = Direct Object or Objects of some prepositions	*Stem + em*	*Same as nom*
N		*Same as nom*	
M/F	Ablative = Objects of some prepositions	*Stem + e*	*Stem + ibus*
N		*Stem + i*	

Day 2, Exercise 3: Fill in the following chart(s):

Which rule tells you "caput, capitis" is neuter? <u>*L-A-N-C-E-T*</u>

Is it i-stem?   ○ Yes   ○ <u>*No*</u>

If yes, which rule? _____

Case	Singular	Plural
Nominative	caput	*capita*
Genitive	*capitis*	*capitum*
Dative	*capiti*	*capitibus*
Accusative	*caput*	*capita*
Ablative	*capite*	*capitibus*

(This exercise is continued on the next page.)

Which rule tells you "dux, ducis" is masculine? **_It is an exception._**

Is it i-stem?   ○ Yes   ○ **_No_**

If yes, which rule? _____

Case	Singular	Plural
Nominative	dux	*duces*
Genitive	*ducis*	*ducum*
Dative	*duci*	*ducibus*
Accusative	*ducem*	*duces*
Ablative	*duce*	*ducibus*

Which rule tells you "panis, panis" is feminine? **_S-O-X_**

Is it i-stem?   ○ **_Yes_**   ○ No

If yes, which rule? **_Nominative ends in is, and it has the same number of syllables in the first and second form._**

Case	Singular	Plural
Nominative	panis	*panes*
Genitive	*panis*	*panium*
Dative	*pani*	*panibus*
Accusative	*panem*	*panes*
Ablative	*pane*	*panibus*

Day 2, Exercise 4: Fill in the chart. The first one is done for you.

Word	Regular/I-Stem	Gender	Case	Number
maria	i-stem	Neut.	Nominative/Accusative	Plural
flumen	*regular*	*Neut.*	*Nom./Acc.*	*Singular*
gentibus	*i-stem*	*Fem.*	*Dative/Ablative*	*Plural*
pastore	*regular*	*Masc.*	*Ablative*	*Singular*

Day 3, Exercise 1: Do a complete synopsis of the verb 'regere'.

A verb that loves its i will keep it, but otherwise it copycats the -ere verbs. It doesn't have to change the "e" to "i" for the present, because it is already an "i." However, it adds the "e" for the past and future, so it can be just like the third conjugation -ere words, but it doesn't lose its "i." It loves its "i." The future possible changes the "e" of the regular to an "a."

	Present	Past	Future Regulars	Future Possibles
1st Singular	*rego*	*regebam*	*regam*	*regam*
2nd Singular	*regis*	*regebas*	*reges*	*regas*
3rd Singular	*regit*	*regebat*	*reget*	*regat*
1st Plural	*regimus*	*regebamus*	*regemus*	*regamus*
2nd Plural	*regitis*	*regebatis*	*regetis*	*regatis*
3rd Plural	*regunt*	*regebant*	*regent*	*regant*

Beginning Latin II - Lesson XXIV

Day 3, Exercise 2: Circle the nominative/subjects, box the genitive/possessives, underline the accusative/direct objects, and dash underline the datives/indirect objects (objects of for). Put parentheses around prepositions and their objects and label the prepositions with a "p". Also, make sure to underline the objects of accusative prepositions.

Before doing this exercises let's go over this in more detail.

Look at your list of prepositions in the vocabulary section.

First, put "p" above the prepositions you find in the below sentences. (See my "p" above "through" and "by" in the example sentence.)

Next find the object of the prepositions. It's the next real word. Make sure you put the parentheses around the whole phrase. See below. I found the object of "through" which was "road". I put a set of parentheses around "through the road". I crossed out "the", of course. I did the same things for "by" the "house". ("House" is the object of "by".)

Finally, look at the vocabulary list to see if those prepositions took the accusative or the ablative. In my example, I saw that "through" took an accusative object. I saw that "by" took an ablative object. So, I underlined the object of "through" but not the object of "by".

Did you notice that I underlined the object when it was accusative, but not ablative? Look at the word "road" below. Notice I underlined it with a single underline. I also use single underlines for accusative/direct objects.

I use single underlines for accusative/direct objects and accusative/objects of prepositions. I use a single underline for all accusatives.

Example: ~~The~~ [man's] (cat) ran (through ~~the~~ road)(by ~~the~~ house).
p p

Here are your sentences:

1. ~~The~~ (girl) sang ~~a~~ song for ~~the~~ mother of [God].

2. (I) walked (into ~~a~~ church.)
p

3. ~~The~~ (man) is calling ~~the~~ horse.

4. (Mary) worked ~~the~~ shift for Teresa.

5. (Sam) wants [Dreyer's] ice cream (from ~~the~~ store.)
p

Review Lesson C

Day 1, Exercise 1: Do a complete synopsis of the verb "munire":

	Present	Past	Future Regulars	Future Possibles
1st Singular	*munio*	*muniebam*	*muniam*	*muniam*
2nd Singular	*munis*	*muniebas*	*munies*	*munias*
3rd Singular	*munit*	*muniebat*	*muniet*	*muniat*
1st Plural	*munimus*	*muniebamus*	*muniemus*	*muniamus*
2nd Plural	*munitis*	*muniebatis*	*munietis*	*muniatis*
3rd Plural	*muniunt*	*muniebant*	*munient*	*muniant*

Day 1, Exercise 2: True or False

laudare..................................to praise	***True***	False
monēre..................................to eat	True	***False***
audire...................................to hear	***True***	False
agere....................................to act	***True***	False
civitas, civitatis.....................state	***True***	False
pax, pacis.............................peace	***True***	False
caput, capitis........................cross	True	***False***
Caesar, Caesaris..................Caesar	***True***	False
diu..a day	True	***False***
lux, lucis..............................law	True	***False***

Day 1, Exercise 3: Do a complete synopsis of the verb "scribere":

	Present	Past	Future Regulars	Future Possibles
1st Singular	scribo	scribebam	scribam	scribam
2nd Singular	scribis	scribebas	scribes	scribas
3rd Singular	scribit	scribebat	scribet	scribat
1st Plural	scribimus	scribebamus	scribemus	scribamus
2nd Plural	scribitis	scribebatis	scribetis	scribatis
3rd Plural	scribunt	scribebant	scribent	scribant

Day 1, Exercise 4: Translate

A. I may run. — *curram*

B. You (singular) will draw. — *trahes*

C. She was learning. — *discebat*

D. You (singular) seek. — *petis*

E. We were acting. — *agebamus*

F. She will send. — *mittet*

G. It may feel. — *sentiat*

H. You (plural) live. — *vivitis*

Day 1, Exercise 5: Fill in the blanks:

	Word	Meaning
1st Singular	malo	I prefer
2nd Singular	mavis	you prefer
3rd Singular	mavult	he prefers
1st Plural	malumus	we prefer
2nd Plural	mavultis	you prefer
3rd Plural	malunt	they prefer

	Word	Meaning
1st Singular	fero	I bear
2nd Singular	fers	you bear
3rd Singular	fert	he bears
1st Plural	ferimus	we bear
2nd Plural	fertis	you bear
3rd Plural	ferunt	they bear

	Word	Meaning
1st Singular	sum	I am
2nd Singular	es	you are
3rd Singular	est	it is
1st Plural	sumus	we are
2nd Plural	estis	you are
3rd Plural	sunt	they are

Day 1, Exercise 6: Find the stem of the following words:

scribere — *scribe*

lux, lucis — *luc*

tentatio, tentationis — *tentation*

civis, civis — *civ*

trahere — *trahe*

Day 2, Exercise 1: Match.

Future Tense Regular *(I will call)* — I call.

Future Tense Possible *(May I call)* — I will call.

Present Tense *(I call)* — I was calling

Past Tense *(I was calling)* — May I call.

Day 2, Exercise 2: True or False

bibere......to drink	**True**	False
edere......to eat	**True**	False
vivere......to conquer	True	**False**
ponere......to place	**True**	False
regere......to rule	**True**	False
non......for a long time	True	**False**
urbs, urbis......citizen	True	**False**
flumen, fluminis......run	True	**False**
Cicero, Ciceronis (m)......Cicero	**True**	False
canis, canis (m/f)......horse	True	**False**
veritas, veritatis......virgin	True	**False**
virgo, virginis......virgin	**True**	False

Day 2, Exercise 3: Match the correct associations.

Subject *(Nominative)*	L-A-N-C-E-T
Possessive *(Genitive)*	ER-R-OR
Neuter Words *(L-A-N-C-E-T)*	Genitive
Feminine Words *(S-O-X)*	Accusative
Indirect Objects/Objects of "for" *(Dative)*	Dative
Direct Objects *(Accusative)*	Nominative
Masculine Words *(ER-R-OR)*	S-O-X

Day 2, Exercise 4: True or False

A noun is i-stem if it…..

Ends in -er or -or in the nominative first form and has the same number of syllables in the first and second form.	True	***False***
Ends in -s or -x in the nominative first form and has a stem that ends in two consonants.	***True***	False
Ends in -al, -ar, or -e in the nominative first form (masculine nouns).	True	***False***

Day 2, Exercise 5: Match the correct associations.

1st Person Plural *(we)*	he, she, it
2nd Person Singular *(you, sing)*	you (sing)
3rd Person Plural *(they)*	I
2nd Person Plural *(you, plural)*	they
1st Person Singular *(I)*	we
3rd Person Singular *(he, she, it)*	you (plural)

Day 2, Exercise 6: Complete the chart for an i-stem word.

Gender	Case	Singular	Plural
M/F	Nominative = Subject	*1st form*	*Stem + es*
N			*Stem + ia*
All	Genitive = Possessive	*2nd form*	*Stem + ium*
All	Dative = Indirect Object	*Stem + i*	*Stem + ibus*
M/F	Accusative = Direct Object or Objects of some prepositions	*Stem + em*	*Same as nom*
N		*Same as nom*	
M/F	Ablative = Objects of some prepositions	*Stem + e*	*Stem + ibus*
N		*Stem + i*	

Day 2, Exercise 7: Fill in the blanks.

	Word	Meaning
1st Singular	nolo	*I am not willing*
2nd Singular	non vis	*you are not willing*
3rd Singular	non vult	*he is not willing*
1st Plural	nolumus	*we are not willing*
2nd Plural	non vultis	*you are not wiling*
3rd Plural	nolunt	*they are not willing*

(This exercise is continued on the next page.)

	Word	Meaning
1st Singular	*potero*	I will be able
2nd Singular	*poteris*	you will be able
3rd Singular	*poterit*	it will be able
1st Plural	*poterimus*	we will be able
2nd Plural	*poteritis*	you will be able
3rd Plural	*poterunt*	they will be able

	Word	Meaning
1st Singular	volo	*I am willing*
2nd Singular	vis	*you are willing*
3rd Singular	vult	*he is willing*
1st Plural	volumus	*we are willing*
2nd Plural	vultis	*you are willing*
3rd Plural	volunt	*they are willing*

Day 3, Exercise 1: Rules

The -ire verbs love their **_i's_**. They also copycat the -ere verbs.

In the present tense, for -ere verbs, you change the "e" of the stem to **_i._**

In the future tense regular, for -ere verbs, you **_leave the stem alone_**.

In the future tense possible, for -ere verbs, you **_change the e to an a_**.

In the past tense, for -ere verbs, you add **_ba_** to the stem and then add the ending.

Day 3, Exercise 2: True or False

vincere....................to conquer	***True***	False
credere....................to believe	***True***	False
ducere....................leader	True	***False***
currere....................to run	***True***	False
mittere....................to catch	True	***False***
tempus, temporis (n)....................time	***True***	False
civis, civis (m/f)....................state	True	***False***
dux, ducis (m)....................leader	***True***	False
lex, legis....................light	True	***False***
saepe....................often	***True***	False

Day 3, Exercise 3: Fill in the chart.

Word	Regular/i-Stem	Gender	Case	Number
gentium	i-stem	Fem	Genitive	Plural
pastore	*regular*	*Masc*	*Ablative*	*Sing*
tempora	*regular*	*Neut*	*Nominative/Accusative*	*Plural*
luci	*regular*	*Fem*	*Dative*	*Sing*

Day 3, Exercise 4: Fill in the blanks.

	Word	Meaning
1st Singular	eram	I was
2nd Singular	eras	you were
3rd Singular	erat	he was
1st Plural	eramus	we were
2nd Plural	eratis	you were
3rd Plural	erant	they were

	Word	Meaning
1st Singular	possum	I am able
2nd Singular	potes	you are able
3rd Singular	potest	he is able
1st Plural	possumus	we are able
2nd Plural	potestis	you are able
3rd Plural	possunt	they are able

	Word	Meaning
1st Singular	*ero*	*I will be*
2nd Singular	*eris*	*you will be*
3rd Singular	*erit*	*it will be*
1st Plural	*erimus*	*we will be*
2nd Plural	*eritis*	*you will be*
3rd Plural	*erunt*	*they will be*

	Word	Meaning
1st Singular	poteram	*I was able*
2nd Singular	poteras	*you were able*
3rd Singular	poterat	*he was able*
1st Plural	poteramus	*we were able*
2nd Plural	poteratis	*you were able*
3rd Plural	poterant	*they were able*

Day 3, Exercise 5: Complete the chart.

Gender	Case	Singular	Plural
M/F	Nominative = Subject	1st form	Stem + es
N			Stem + a
All	Genitive = Possessive	2nd form	Stem + um
All	Dative = Indirect Object	Stem + i	Stem + ibus
M/F	Accusative = Direct Object or Objects of some prepositions	Stem + em	Same as nom
N		Same as nom	Same as nom
All	Ablative = Objects of some prepositions	Stem + e	Stem + ibus

Day 4, Exercise 1: True or False

defendere..................................to conquer	True	*False*	
scribere.....................................to write	*True*	False	
sentire.......................................to feel	*True*	False	
munire.......................................to feel	True	*False*	
dicere..to speak	*True*	False	
rex, regis (m)...........................lord	True	*False*	
crux, crucis...............................cross	*True*	False	
dolor, doloris.............................law	True	*False*	
panis, panis (m).........................pain	True	*False*	
mons, montis (m).......................mountain	*True*	False	
homo, hominis (m)......................man	*True*	False	
arbor, arboris (f).........................fountain	True	*False*	
sol, solis (m)..............................summit	True	*False*	

Day 4, Exercise 2: Decline the following nouns by completing the chart.

Word: caritas, caritatis   Is it i-stem?   ○ Yes   ○ **_No_**

If yes, which rule: _____

Gender: ○ Masculine   ○ **_Feminine_**   ○ Neuter

Case	Singular	Plural
Nominative	caritas	*caritates*
Genitive	*caritatis*	*caritatum*
Dative	*caritati*	*caritatibus*
Accusative	*caritatem*	*caritates*
Ablative	*caritate*	*caritatibus*

Word: mare, maris   Is it i-stem?   ○ **_Yes_**   ○ No

If yes, which rule: ***It's a neuter word that ends in "e"***

Gender: ○ Masculine   ○ Feminine   ○ **_Neuter_**

Case	Singular	Plural
Nominative	mare	*maria*
Genitive	*maris*	*marium*
Dative	*mari*	*maribus*
Accusative	mare	*maria*
Ablative	*mari*	*maribus*

Day 4, Exercise 3: True or False

trahere....................................to draw	**_True_**	False
gerere....................................to write	True	**_False_**
discere....................................to teach	True	**_False_**
cedere....................................to yield	**_True_**	False
petere....................................to seek	**_True_**	False
mare, maris (m)....................................horse	True	**_False_**
pastor, pastoris....................................pasture	True	**_False_**
gens, gentis....................................tribe	**_True_**	False
libertas, libertatis....................................love	True	**_False_**
caritas, caritatis....................................liberty	True	**_False_**
fons, fontis (m)....................................tribe	True	**_False_**

Day 4, Exercise 4: Give the meaning of the following indeclinables.

non	**_not_**	diu	**_for a long time_**
saepe	**_often_**	bene	**_well_**
in (ablative)	**_in, on_**	in (accusative)	**_into, onto_**
ad (accusative)	**_to, toward_**	trans (accusative)	**_across_**
per (accusative)	**_through_**	contra (accusative)	**_against_**
ante (accusative)	**_before_**	post (accusative)	**_after_**
a, ab (ablative)	**_by_**	cum (ablative)	**_with_**
e, ex (ablative)	**_out of_**	de (ablative)	**_from, down from_**